THE
PSYCHOLOGY
OF **TRADING**

THE
PSYCHOLOGY
OF **TRADING**

Strengthen Your Mindset and
Refine Your Trading Process

SUNIL GURJAR

JAICO PUBLISHING HOUSE

Ahmedabad Bangalore Chennai
Delhi Hyderabad Kolkata Mumbai

Published by Jaico Publishing House
A-2 Jash Chambers, 7-A Sir Phirozshah Mehta Road
Fort, Mumbai - 400 001
jaicopub@jaicobooks.com
www.jaicobooks.com

THE PSYCHOLOGY OF TRADING
ISBN 978-93-49358-06-5

First Jaico Impression: 2025

Page design and layout by Inosoft Systems, Delhi

Printed by
Parksons Graphics Pvt. Ltd., Mumbai

CONTENTS

SECTION III

IMPROVING YOUR SYSTEM

SECTION IV

THE UNENDING GAME: CHALLENGES
BEYOND PROFITABILITY

AUTHOR'S NOTE

This book is all about trading psychology — but not in a theoretical way. I am talking about real, practical, and actionable insights. My idea is not to share what should work in the market. It is about showing what has worked for me — a full-time trader who has been through the ups and downs and emerge with hard-earned lessons.

You can read this book cover to cover (which I recommend, since the ideas build on each other). But I also know that sometimes, you just want to flip to a page and get something useful right away. That is why each chapter stands on its own — you can go deep when you want to or grab a quick insight when you need it.

Everything I am sharing through this book comes from my own experience — the mistakes, the lessons, and the strategies that actually made a difference. I am not a psychologist, and I will not pretend to be one. I am just someone who has faced the mental battles of trading and found ways to make the game a little easier.

This book is all about practical stuff you can actually use — things that can help you trade better, and maybe even navigate life better. So let us dive in. Whether you are here to strengthen your mindset, refine your process, or just stay sane in this wild game, I am glad you are here.

This book is a reflection of my journey, and I hope it helps you on yours.

INTRODUCTION

Experienced traders often say, "Trading is the hardest way to make easy money." This is not because trading itself is complicated — it is because of the mental strength required to master it. Most people can understand the technical side of trading, no matter which strategy they follow. But they still struggle to match their mindset with the market. There is this invisible force that holds them back, no matter what they do.

In such situations, many traders start questioning themselves: "Am I not smart enough?" or "Maybe I am just not meant for this." The simple solution I have found to these problems is relying on trading psychology. It is all about managing thoughts and emotions since they directly impact your decisions in the market. But then you wonder if psychology alone is enough to succeed in trading. Can you just control your emotions and expect results? If you read a book by a psychologist instead of a trader, they might say yes. But the reality is not that simple. Let us figure out why.

SOFT EDGE VS HARD EDGE

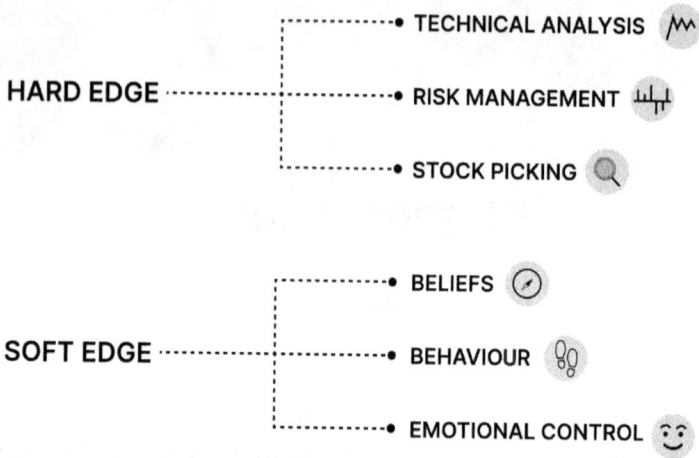

HARD EDGE
- TECHNICAL ANALYSIS
- RISK MANAGEMENT
- STOCK PICKING

SOFT EDGE
- BELIEFS
- BEHAVIOUR
- EMOTIONAL CONTROL

To succeed in trading, you need two types of edge— a soft edge and a hard edge. The hard edge, which is essentially your trading strategy, comprises your technical skills which include technical analysis (TA), fundamental analysis (FA), chart patterns, setups, and risk management. All these are measurable skills that directly impact your trading results. If you learn a trading setup or improve your risk management, you will definitely see better results right away.

The soft edge, on the other hand, is your psychological approach—your beliefs, behaviour, emotional control, and overall mindset. Unlike the hard edge, which is easy to measure and quickly affects your results—the soft edge is more subtle. It is about discipline, handling stress, and keeping a strong mindset. While it may not seem that important at first, it plays a huge role in the long-term success of a trader. It is much easier to track progress related to the hard edge because it has a clear and immediate impact on your trades. You can see if your technical skills are improving by looking at your results. But the soft edge is a bit difficult to measure because its effects take time and are often only noticeable when you actively work on your approach. Hence, most people either ignore it, or do not work on it enough to see noticeable results. For example, staying calm in a rough market will not show instant results, but over time, it helps you avoid big mistakes and keeps your trading consistent.

THE THREE PILLARS OF SUCCESSFUL TRADING

Some traders say that having a strong trading strategy — your hard edge — is all that matters. To them, everything else is just noise. Others believe that psychology is the key — if your mindset is strong, you can still perform well, even if your technical skills are weak. Then there are those who say that risk management is the ultimate weapon of a trader, claiming that if you manage risk well, you can survive in the market no matter what. So, who's right?

The truth is, they are all right — and wrong — at the same time. If you believe in only one of these three theories and neglect the others it is very similar to trying to balance a table on just one leg. No matter how strong that leg is, the table will still fall.

To succeed in trading, you need a combination of all three:

- A trading strategy with a long-term positive expectancy.
- A strong mindset to handle the ups and downs.
- Good risk management to protect your capital.

Good Trading Psychology

Good Trading Strategy

Good Risk Management

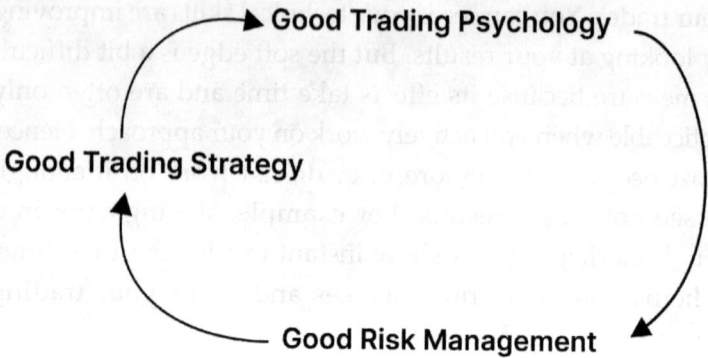

In this book, I will focus mainly on trading psychology since most people ignore it. But remember, to truly improve as a trader, you need to develop all three areas together — not just one.

THE BEHAVIOUR GAP

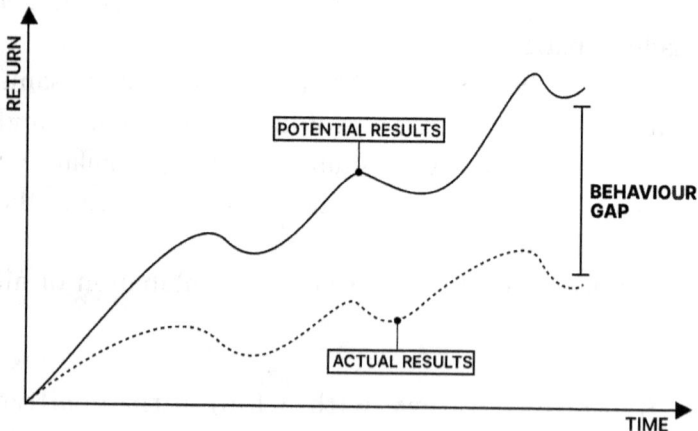

RETURN

POTENTIAL RESULTS

BEHAVIOUR GAP

ACTUAL RESULTS

TIME

Most traders spend their early years focusing only on technical skills, ignoring the psychological side of trading. As a result, they get close to profitability — but never quite reach it. This is called the behaviour gap. It is the difference between the results a trader could achieve based on their skills and the actual results they get due to psychological barriers. A trader might have a solid strategy, great risk management, and a deep understanding of the market. But if they cannot control their emotions, they end up making mistakes—deviating from their plan because of fear, greed, impatience, or overconfidence. This leads to poor trading performance. To fix this, many traders think they just need better strategies or more technical skills. They keep tweaking their setups, hoping that is the missing piece. But the real problem is not their strategy—it is their own behaviour. No matter how much you refine your technical skills, you will not achieve consistent profitability if you do not address your mental roadblocks.

Unlike charts, which stay the same, understanding yourself is an ongoing process. You learn from mistakes, adjust, and keep improving. Traders who take the time to work on their mindset have a huge advantage. They make better decisions and handle market ups and downs more effectively.

In this book, we will explore practical ways to take control of your trading and close the behavioural gap.

Trading success has got nothing to do with being lucky.

At first, trading looks like an easy way to make money. The idea of making money just by clicking some buttons is tempting. But the reality is very different.

When you see traders showing off their big returns, remember—many more are losing money as trading is essentially a zero-sum game; for every winner, there is a loser. The real question is: How do you survive and thrive in such a tough environment?

Many traders start with big dreams but quickly fall into "comfortable numbness." They trade out of habit, making money for their brokers but not for themselves.

They get stuck in a cycle—losing money, feeling discouraged, forgetting about it, and then repeating the same mistakes.

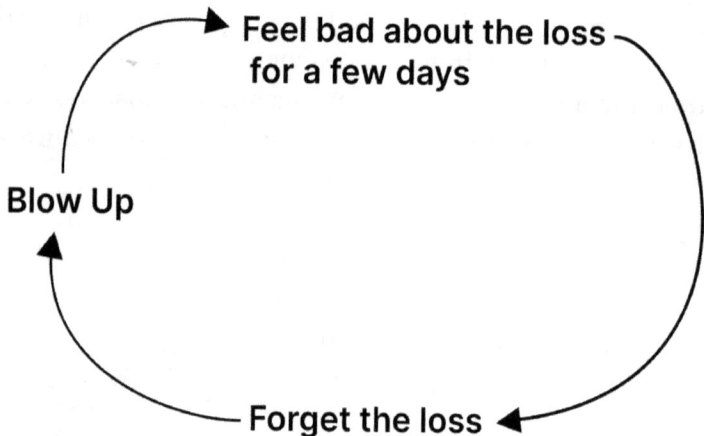

Feel bad about the loss
for a few days

Blow Up

Forget the loss

While the ultimate goal is to make money, some traders start chasing the excitement of trading itself rather than following a process. This turns them into gamblers, relying on luck instead of discipline. They keep believing their luck will change, but without changing their approach, their results stay the same.

**Doing the same thing over and over and
expecting different results is insanity.**

Bad habits like overtrading, trading without a plan, and making impulsive decisions lead to repeated losses. Many traders realise too late that what they thought was "gaining experience" was just losing money in the same way, again and again.

If you have a stable job or business, it is easy to keep losing money in trading without feeling the impact. But those without this safety net often quit, blaming bad luck instead of recognising their mistakes. The real issue here is the mindset and process. If you keep thinking and trading the same way, you will keep getting the same results. Many traders underestimate how hard trading is. They jump in, competing against skilled professionals, without proper preparation.

This might sound harsh, but it is a reality check. Trading offers freedom — no boss, no limits on earnings — but getting there takes serious effort and discipline. So, ask yourself: Are you truly serious about trading? For most, success will require a complete shift in mindset and approach. You will need to embrace discipline, patience, continuous learning, and a solid trading plan.

Trading is not about luck — it is about consistent effort and smart strategies. If you are willing to make these changes, you can turn trading from a frustrating struggle into a rewarding pursuit. The road will not be easy, but with dedication, financial freedom is absolutely possible.

SECTION I

UNDERSTANDING THE TRADER'S MINDSET

"The mind is everything. What you think, you become."
— Buddha

In this first section, we explore what really makes a trader tick — the mindset. It is all about the powerful emotions that come into play with every decision you make: fear, greed, and that burning desire to win. These emotions can either push you toward success or pull you off course; knowing how to handle them is key.

We will also take a closer look at those sneaky cognitive biases that can mess with your thinking and lead to irrational choices. By getting a good grasp on these psychological forces, you will be in a better position to develop a mindset that not only supports your trading goals but also helps you navigate the markets with more confidence.

ONE

FEAR

Have you ever felt nervous or unsure while making a trading decision? If yes, you are not alone. Fear is something every trader experiences at some point. It can make you hesitate, second-guess yourself, or even take actions that go against your own plan. But fear does not have to control your trading.

In this chapter, we will take a closer look at how fear affects your decisions and, more importantly, how you can manage it. Once you understand fear and learn to handle it better, you will feel more confident in your trades and improve your overall performance.

WHAT IS FEAR IN TRADING?

Fear in trading is that uneasy feeling you get when things seem uncertain or risky. Imagine driving through thick fog. You know your destination, but because you cannot see clearly, you slow down, hesitate, or even stop out of fear of what lies ahead. That is exactly how fear works in trading—it clouds your judgment and makes decision-making harder.

Most of the time, you may experience fear from worrying about losing money, making mistakes, or missing out on opportunities. It is completely normal, and every trader faces it. But the real question is—how do you handle it?

Fear can show up in many ways while trading. Maybe you hesitate before entering a trade or you exit too early because you are scared of losing profits. Or, you avoid trading altogether after a loss, afraid of making another mistake.

Before you can overcome fear, you need to recognise when and why it happens. In the subsequent sections, I will break down different types of fear and show you how to deal with them, step by step.

Here are some common types of fear that traders face in their trading journey.

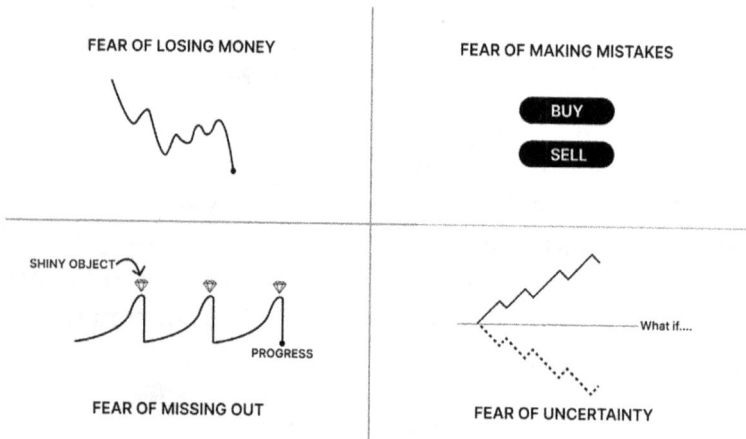

1. Fear of Losing Money

This is one of the biggest fears traders face. Let us be honest— nobody likes to lose, whether in life or in the markets. People love sharing their wins. But failures? Not so much. Losing money often feels like a personal failure, making it even harder to accept.

In trading, this fear can be paralysing.

Markets are unpredictable, and when real money is on the line, the pressure increases. You might hesitate before entering a trade, second-guess your decisions, or even hold on to losing trades too long, hoping they will turn around.

The problem? Fear of losing money can lead to even bigger losses. If you let fear control your decisions, you might miss good opportunities, exit too soon, or take unnecessary risks just to recover losses. In the end, it is not just about money – it is about how fear affects your mindset and trading discipline.

2. Fear of Making Mistakes

This fear is closely linked to the fear of losing money – it is almost like a by-product of it. Traders worry about making the wrong move, so they hesitate, overanalyse, and second-guess every trade.

Why does this happen? Because mistakes come with consequences. A bad trade can mean lost money, shattered confidence, and the frustration of knowing you "should have" done something differently. Instead of accepting that mistakes are part of the process, many traders freeze, overwhelmed by uncertainty.

The irony? The more you fear making mistakes, the more likely you are to make them. Overthinking can lead to missed opportunities, poor timing, or impulsive decisions just to escape the pressure. The key is not to avoid mistakes – but to learn from them without letting fear control your actions.

3. Fear of Missing Out

The fear of missing out (FOMO) is one of the biggest psychological traps in trading. It is that anxious feeling you get when you see a stock skyrocketing, and you think, "If I don't jump in now, I'll miss out on huge profits!" This fear pushes traders to act impulsively — chasing stocks just because they are trending, overleveraging in the hopes of quick gains, or taking trades that do not align with their strategy. Instead of making well-thought-out decisions, they act out of fear, worried that they will be left behind while others make money.

The problem? More often than not, FOMO-driven trades lead to poor outcomes. By the time most traders jump in, the move is already over, or they take on unnecessary risks.

Learning to control FOMO is crucial because in trading, patience often pays off more than impulsiveness.

4. Fear of Uncertainty

Humans crave certainty. We like to know what is going to happen next. But in trading, certainty does not exist. No matter how much analysis you do, how many indicators you add to your chart, or how many opinions you gather from others — you can never be 100% sure of an outcome. Every trade is a coin flip. It can go in your favour, or it can go against you. And that is hard for many traders to accept. This discomfort with the unknown often leads to hesitation, overanalysing, or seeking false reassurance before making a move. Some traders even avoid taking trades altogether, hoping for the "perfect setup" that guarantees success — which does not exist.

But here is the truth: trading is a game of probabilities, not certainties. The key is not to eliminate uncertainty (because you cannot) but to learn how to operate within it. When you accept that uncertainty is part of the process, you free yourself from the fear that holds you back. Instead of trying to predict the future, you focus on executing your strategy, managing risk, and making decisions based on logic, not fear.

FEAR'S BEHAVIOURAL MANIFESTATION

Fear does not just stay in your head—it shows up in the way you trade. It influences your decisions, reactions, and even the way you see the market.

Here are some of the most common ways fear manifests in trading behaviour:

1. Hesitation

Fear makes traders hesitate, keeping them from acting when they should. You may see a setup, analyse it, and even feel confident about it—but then the doubts creep in—"what if I am wrong? What if the market moves against me?" So you wait. You look for more confirmation, second-guess yourself, or overanalyse the trade. By the time you finally decide, the opportunity is gone—the market has already moved, and you are left watching from the sidelines, frustrated and kicking yourself for not taking action earlier.

Hesitation can be especially damaging because it builds a cycle of self-doubt. The more you hesitate, the more you reinforce the idea that you cannot trust yourself to act decisively. And in trading, decisiveness is key.

2. Panic Selling

Fear can push traders into making impulsive decisions, and one of the most common ones is panic selling, that is, dumping positions out of sheer fear rather than a well-thought-out strategy.

Imagine the market suddenly drops, and your positions start bleeding. Your heart races, your mind panics, and all you can think about is stopping the pain. So, you hit the sell button. You tell yourself you are cutting losses, but in reality, you are reacting emotionally, not logically.

The problem? Markets are unpredictable. Many times, after panic-driven selling, the market rebounds — often right after you have exited. Instead of making a calculated decision, you have locked in losses that could have been avoided if you had stayed calm and followed your plan. Panic selling is dangerous because it reinforces fear. Once you act on fear, your brain remembers it as a survival response, making it more likely you will panic again in the future. The key to avoiding such a situation is having a solid plan and trusting it, even when emotions try to take over.

3. Overcautiousness

Fear does not just make traders panic — it can also make them too careful. Being cautious is good, but when fear takes over, traders become so risk-averse that they avoid opportunities altogether or set overly conservative trading parameters. Think about this: You enter a trade but immediately set a very tight stop-loss because you are scared of losing money. The trade barely moves before hitting your stop, closing you out with a small loss — only for the market to then move exactly as you predicted. Or maybe you hesitate to take any trades at all, waiting for the "perfect setup" that never comes. The fear of losing keeps you on the sidelines, watching as others capitalise on the very opportunities you were considering.

While risk management is crucial, overcautiousness can become a hidden form of self-sabotage. Trading requires a balance — protecting yourself from unnecessary risk while still allowing room for opportunity. The goal is not to avoid losing, but to manage risk in a way that lets you stay in the game long enough to win.

4. Analysis Paralysis

Fear can also trap traders in a never-ending cycle of overthinking. Instead of taking action, they get stuck in an endless loop of research, chart analysis, and second-guessing. This is called analysis paralysis—when fear of making a mistake keeps you from making any decision at all.

Picture this: You spend hours scanning charts, watching indicators, and checking news updates, convinced that you just need one more confirmation before entering a trade. But by the time you finally feel ready, the opportunity has passed, and the market has already moved without you. Or maybe you keep switching between strategies, doubting every decision you make. You hesitate, waiting for the "perfect setup" that never comes, while other traders—less burdened by doubt—are out there executing their trades.

Overanalysing does not eliminate risk—it just delays the inevitable. At some point, you have to trust your system and take action, understanding that no trade is ever 100% certain. Trading success comes from making calculated decisions, managing risk, and learning from both wins and losses—not from waiting for the impossible guarantee of certainty.

WHY DO WE EXPERIENCE FEAR IN TRADING?

Fear is a natural and deeply ingrained human emotion. It evolved as a survival mechanism, helping our ancestors avoid danger and react quickly to threats. Those who were more responsive to fear and cautious were more likely to survive, leading to the development of strong neural pathways in our brains that trigger fear responses. While fear was useful for escaping predators in the wild, it does not always serve us well in trading, where success depends on rational decision-making rather than instinctive reactions.

In markets, fear can cloud judgment, cause hesitation, and lead to emotional decision-making—all of which can hurt a trader's performance.

Understanding the evolutionary roots of fear helps traders see why they react the way they do in high-pressure situations. And while fear cannot be completely eliminated, you can train yourself to manage it better so that it does not control your actions.

Every trader, no matter how experienced, encounters fear. The difference between successful and struggling traders is not whether they feel fear—it is how they respond to it. To build the right mindset and minimise the impact of fear on your trading, you need a strong foundation. Here are a few key principles that will help you develop the confidence to navigate the markets without letting fear take over.

1. Understand the probabilistic nature of the game

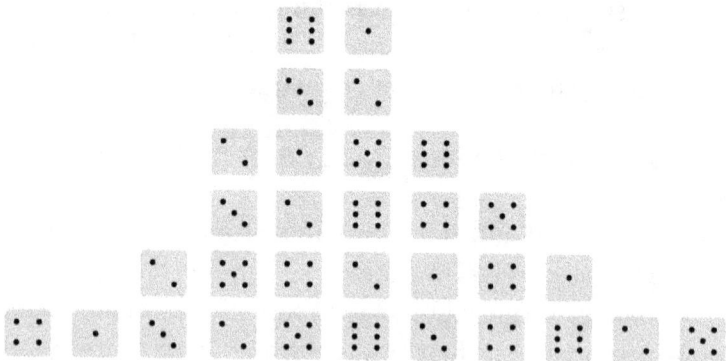

One of the most effective ways to reduce fear in trading—whether it is the fear of losing, the fear of entering new trades, or the fear of uncertainty—is to fully grasp that trading is a probabilistic business.

"A trader should think in probabilities and ignore the short-term noise in their outcomes." Sounds simple, right? But when you are in the middle of a rough patch, staring at multiple losses in a row, these words do not feel very comforting. That is because knowing something is not the same as deeply understanding it. To truly overcome fear, you need to internalise the probabilistic nature of trading. This means rewiring your mindset to see each trade as just one event in a long series, where the outcome of any single trade is far less important than your overall edge playing out over time. When you start thinking this way, losses stop feeling like personal failures and start becoming what they actually are — a normal and expected part of the process. The better you understand this, the less likely it is that fear will dictate your decisions, and the more you will be able to stay calm, focused, and consistent in your approach.

2. Detach yourself from trading outcomes

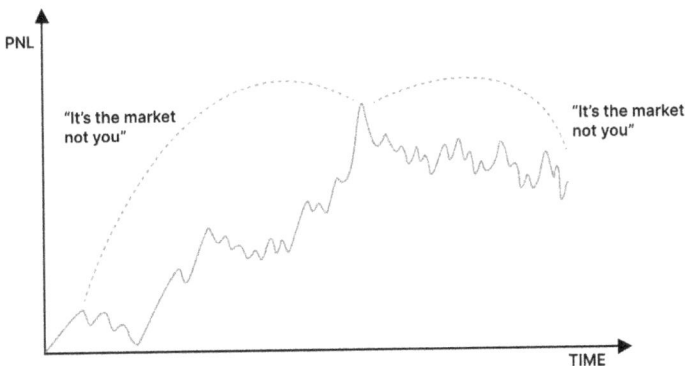

Traders often struggle with fear and stress because they tie their self-worth to their trading results. When a trade goes well, they feel on top of the world—validated and confident. But when a trade goes south, it is a hit to their self-esteem, triggering self-doubt and frustration. This emotional roller coaster is fuelled by the brain's natural aversion to loss and the mistaken belief that trading outcomes define personal value.

The truth is, your worth has nothing to do with your profit and loss. But when trading becomes the center of your world, it is easy to feel like your success—or failure—in the market defines you. That is why it is so important to separate yourself from your results. Put simply: get a life. If trading is the only thing you have going for you, every win or loss will feel monumental. But when you build a life outside trading—one filled with hobbies, relationships, and personal growth—you create emotional balance.

A bad trade will not ruin your day, and a good trade will not be the only thing that makes you feel accomplished. So, diversify your life just like you would a portfolio. Find things that bring you joy other than trading. Pick up a hobby, spend time with family and friends, or do something that makes you feel good just for the sake of it. When your happiness is not solely dependent on your performance in the markets, the emotional swings start to level out. At the end of the day, trading is just one part of who you are—not the whole story. And when you stop letting it define your worth, you will trade with more clarity, confidence, and peace of mind.

3. Develop an abundance mindset

The fear of missing out on potential opportunities is one of the biggest emotional traps in trading. It makes you feel like if you do not jump in right now, you will never get another chance. You either end up sitting on the sidelines, watching the market make big moves without you, or you chase trades that do not fit your strategy—both of which can wreck your progress.

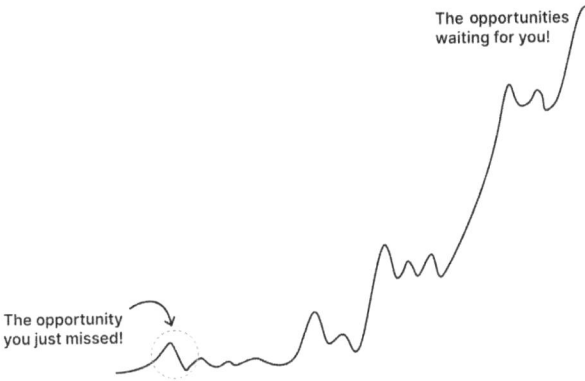

The opportunities waiting for you!

The opportunity you just missed!

But here is the truth: the market is not going anywhere. There will always be more opportunities. I have personally missed some of the biggest moves in the market, and yet, I have still been able to exceed my own expectations as a trader. That experience taught me one of the most important lessons—opportunity is endless, and believing in that makes all the difference.

When you truly adopt an abundance mindset, missing one trade does not shake you. You do not spiral into frustration or chase setups out of desperation. Instead, you stay level-headed, knowing that the market will keep offering new chances. I have seen traders get so caught up in the regret of missing a move that they blinded themselves to the other opportunities right in front of them. Their negative self-talk clouded their judgment, leading to bad decisions and even bigger losses.

The key is to remind yourself: there will always be another trade. When you let go of the fear of missing out and trust in the endless flow of opportunities, you will trade with more patience, clarity, and confidence.

4. Mechanical rules for the win

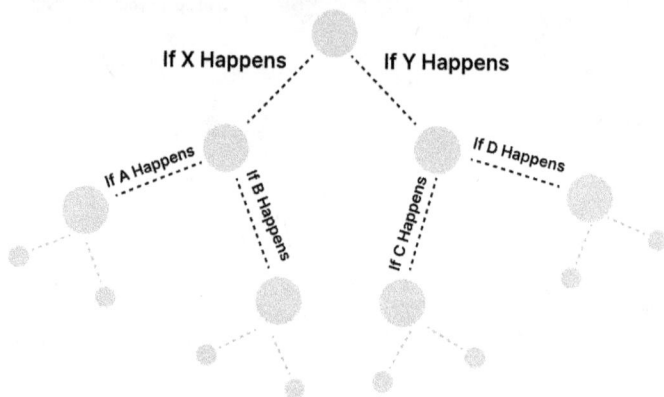

If X Happens   If Y Happens

If A Happens   If D Happens

If B Happens

If C Happens

A lot of the fear and uncertainty traders feel comes from not having a solid plan. You might think you understand your system, but executing it in real-time is a whole different challenge.

When the markets are moving fast, second-guessing yourself can be disastrous. That is why having a clear, mechanical approach is crucial. You need to know exactly what to buy, when to buy it, and how much to buy — without hesitation. You should also have a plan for different market conditions, so you are never caught off guard.

Think of it this way: when the market opens at 9:15, you are just the employee executing the plan that your boss (your logical, clear-headed self from the previous market close) already set in place. The goal is to think less and act more. At its core, trading is about reducing complex decisions into simple, black-and-white rules. The clearer your system, the less room fear has to creep in.

5. Conquering fear for personal and trading growth

Each wall of fear is bigger than the last, but with every leap, your ability to break through grows even faster.

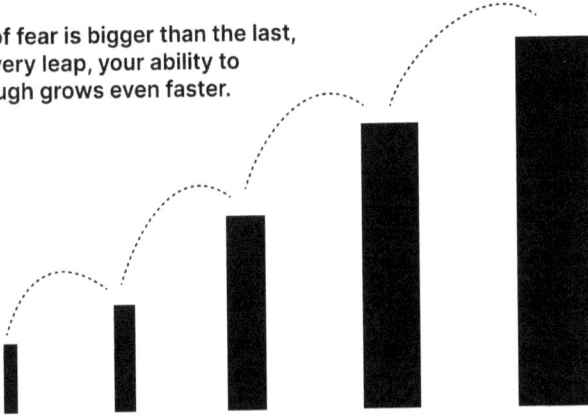

Overcoming fear in trading is like climbing a mountain—difficult, exhausting, and full of moments where you question whether you should turn back. But once you push through, you come out stronger, more capable, and better prepared for future challenges. Conquering fear is not just about becoming a better trader; it is about evolving as a person. When you learn to manage fear, you develop resilience. You stop reacting impulsively to every market fluctuation and instead start responding with logic and discipline. This shift does not just help in trading—it carries over into your life. You become more patient, more adaptable, and more confident in handling uncertainty.

Every time you face fear head-on, whether it is hesitating to take a trade, dealing with a losing streak, or resisting the urge to panic sell, you are building mental toughness. And the stronger your mind becomes, the better you will perform—not just in the market, but in every aspect of life.

6. Boosting confidence

Facing your fears head-on makes you trust yourself more. The more you deal with fear, the more confident you become. In trading, confidence means making decisions without second-guessing yourself. When you believe in your skills, you will not hesitate or panic—you will take action based on logic, not fear.

7. Sharpening emotional skills

Dealing with fear makes you emotionally stronger. Trading is full of ups and downs, and if you can stay calm under pressure, you will make better decisions. When the market is going crazy, traders who control their emotions avoid panic moves. Staying cool helps you think clearly and stick to your plan instead of making rash decisions.

8. Making better choices

When you stop letting fear control you, your decisions become more logical and less emotional. Instead of reacting impulsively, you start weighing risks and rewards calmly. Traders who manage fear well do not chase trades out of FOMO or exit too early out of panic. They stick to their strategy, leading to more consistent and profitable results.

9. Building resilience

Overcoming fear makes you mentally tougher. Instead of breaking down after a loss, you learn from it and keep going. Traders who build resilience understand that losses are just part of the game. They do not let setbacks shake them—they adapt, improve, and come back stronger.

10. The bigger picture

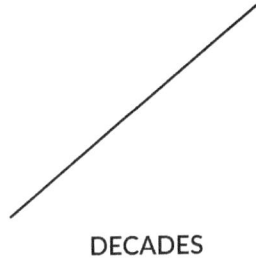

DAYS

DECADES

Overcoming fear in trading is not just about making better trades—it shapes you as a person. As you build confidence, emotional control, and resilience, these qualities spill over into other areas of your life. The discipline and mental strength you develop in trading can help you succeed in everything else you do.

Fear is a big challenge in trading, just like in life. But with a solid trading plan, emotional control, continuous learning, and experience, you can turn fear into a tool for growth.

At the end of the day, overcoming fear is not just about becoming a better trader—it is about becoming a stronger, more resilient person. And that is a journey worth taking, because the benefits go far beyond trading, shaping a more balanced and fulfilling life.

CHAPTER SUMMARY

FEAR

FEAR MAKES YOU HESITATE

FEAR OF LOSING IS NATURAL

SMALL POSITION SIZE HELPS

FEAR INCREASES IN UNCERTAINITY

ACCEPT LOSSES AS PART OF THE GAME

TRADE SMALL

CLEAR PLAN

FOCUS ON EXECUTION

2

GREED

"Greed is a fire that starts with a spark of desire but soon grows into a blaze, consuming all reason and turning contentment to ashes."

Traders often experience their biggest losses right after a winning streak.

Why? Simple answer — greed. It makes you want more — more wins, more trades, more profits. It can be just as dangerous as fear, if not worse. It pushes you to take reckless risks, overtrade, and stray from your strategy. Like a gambler chasing a hot streak, a trader driven by greed can quickly spiral into losses.

But just like fear, greed can be managed. In this chapter, we will break down how greed creeps into trading and go over practical ways to keep it under control.

UNDERSTANDING GREED IN TRADING

Greed is that intense craving for more — more profits, more wins, more success. In trading, it kicks in when you see the possibility of making big money. That excitement can blind you to your own biases and flaws in your approach. It makes you chase every opportunity, even the bad ones.

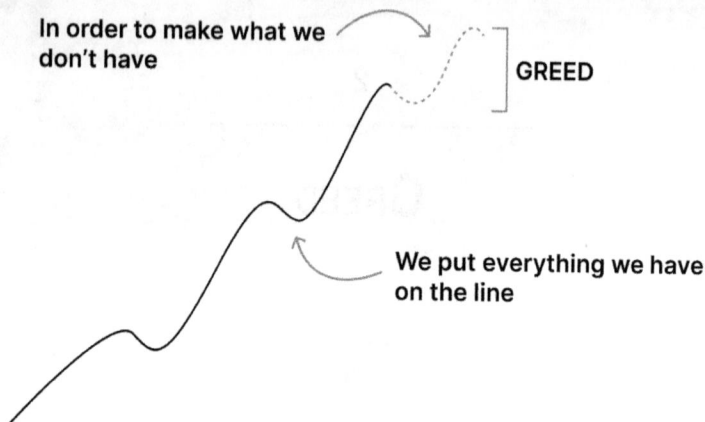

In order to make what we don't have

GREED

We put everything we have on the line

You start ignoring your trading plan, taking bigger risks, and holding on to winning trades for too long, hoping for even more gains. Greed can fuel ambition, but if left unchecked, it can just as easily lead to disaster. Managing it is key to long-term success.

COMMON TYPES OF GREED IN TRADING

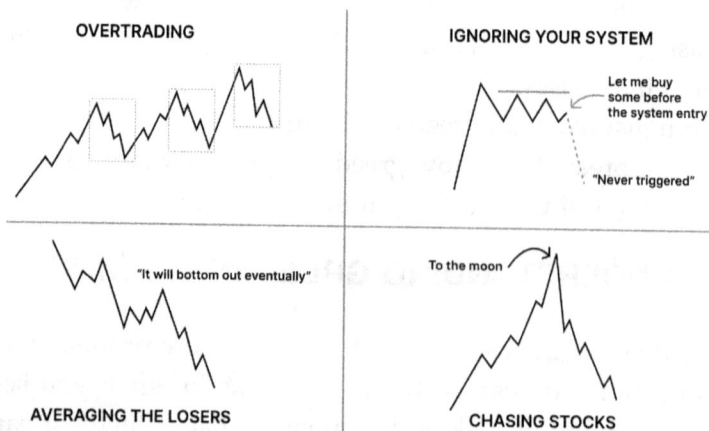

OVERTRADING

IGNORING YOUR SYSTEM

Let me buy some before the system entry

"Never triggered"

"It will bottom out eventually"

To the moon

AVERAGING THE LOSERS

CHASING STOCKS

1. Overtrading

One of the biggest signs of greed in trading is overtrading — jumping into too many trades, even the ones that do not fit your strategy. The fear of missing out and seeing others make big money can push you into impulsive decisions.

But here is the problem: overtrading drains your capital fast. It racks up transaction costs, leads to burnout, and can put you in a hole that is hard to climb out of — even for experienced traders.

The key is to stay disciplined and stick to your process.

2. Ignoring your system

A strong trading plan is key to long-term success, but greed can tempt you to break your own rules for the chance of bigger returns. Maybe you take a trade that does not fit your strategy, risk more than usual, or hold on too long, hoping for just a little more. The danger comes when you justify it as a "one-time thing."

The moment you make an exception, you create a habit of bending the rules. In trading, bad habits can be costly. As Aristotle put it, *"We are what we repeatedly do."* If you want to be a disciplined trader, you have to trade with discipline — every single time.

3. Averaging down on losing positions

When driven by greed, you might be tempted to average down on a losing position, thinking, "It is already below my cost, so I have to hold. It has to go up, right?"

First, there is no "have to" in trading. You either take a loss or you do not — it is always a decision. Averaging down is risky because it violates a fundamental rule: cut losses quickly. By buying more of a stock that is already falling, you are doubling down on a poor performer, increasing your exposure, and potentially compounding your losses if the decline continues.

Another thing to factor in is the opportunity cost. Every rupee stuck in a failing trade is a rupee not working in a better opportunity. Holding on to losers can weigh down your overall performance more than you realise.

4. Chasing the hot opportunities

Greed can also make you chase the market, jumping into trades out of FOMO rather than solid analysis. This often means entering too late at bad prices — and worse, it can lead to impulsive decisions like micromanaging your trades, which is a recipe for disaster.

HOW GREED AFFECTS YOUR BEHAVIOUR

Greed can quietly sabotage your trading, often without you even realising it. Here are some common ways it creeps into your decisions:

1. Holding on to winning positions too long

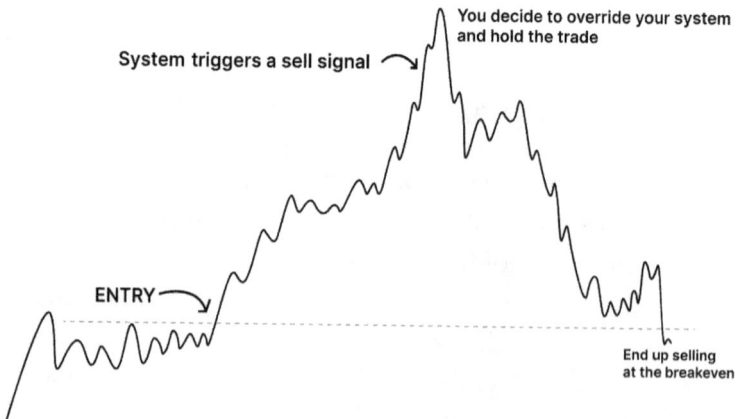

You decide to override your system and hold the trade

System triggers a sell signal

ENTRY

End up selling at the breakeven

One of the most common ways greed creeps in is by holding on to winning positions too long, hoping for even bigger gains—even when your trading plan says otherwise.

While letting profits run is important, there is a fine line between maximising gains and overstaying your welcome in a trade. Your exits should be part of a well-defined system, not a last-minute decision driven by emotions. A structured approach, based on data from a large sample of trades, helps you stay disciplined and avoid greed-driven mistakes. Ignoring your exit strategy can be costly. If you keep holding past your planned exit, you risk turning a profitable system into a losing one—this is how edges erode.

2. Taking on excessive risk

Greed can push you to take on excessive risk, especially when you see others making big gains and feel like you are falling behind. That urge to catch up can lead to impulsive trades—ones you would not normally take. At first, it might feel exciting. A few wins can boost your confidence, making you take even bigger risks. But that excitement is short-lived. If the market turns against you, that same overconfidence can spiral into frustration, leading to even more impulsive decisions—ones that can hurt your trading system in the long run.

Why do we experience greed in trading? Greed, like fear, is deeply rooted in our psychology and evolutionary past. In the context of trading, greed can be understood through several psychological and emotional factors. Here are a few:

i. Evolutionary roots

The drive for more—whether food, shelter, or security—was essential for our ancestors' survival. Those who sought extra resources had a better chance of making it and passing on their genes.That same instinct is still hardwired into us today, but in modern contexts like trading, it often shows up as greed.

ii. Dopamine and reward systems

The human brain is wired to seek rewards, and trading can trigger a dopamine rush — the same neurotransmitter linked to pleasure and reinforcement. A winning trade releases dopamine, creating a sense of euphoria and strengthening the urge to chase more gains.This dopamine-driven high can be addictive, pushing you to take bigger risks in pursuit of that same feeling — often at the cost of sound decision-making.

iii. Social comparison

In trading, as in life, we naturally compare ourselves to others. Seeing other traders boast about big wins can spark envy and greed, making you feel like you need to keep up. This social comparison often leads to unrealistic expectations and reckless decisions as you chase results that may not even be sustainable.

ON MANAGING GREED

Recognising and managing greed is essential for long-term success in trading. Here are some strategies to help you keep greed in check:

1. Stick to your trading plan

One of the best ways to manage greed is to have a trading plan — and more importantly, to stick to it. A well-defined plan lays out your process, including entry and exit rules, risk management, and position sizing. Following it helps you stay disciplined and avoid impulsive decisions driven by greed.

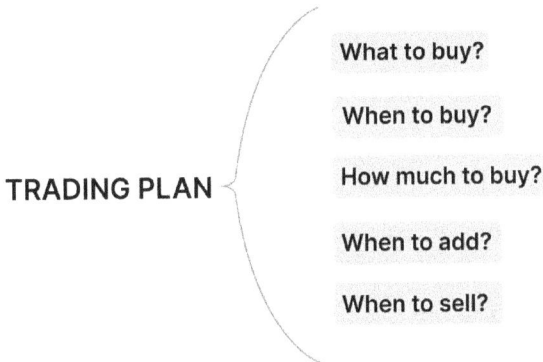

TRADING PLAN

- What to buy?
- When to buy?
- How much to buy?
- When to add?
- When to sell?

2. Set realistic goals

Setting realistic and achievable trading goals can help you stay focused and avoid the temptation to chase after unrealistic profits. Break your goals down into smaller, manageable milestones, and celebrate your progress along the way.

3. Use proper risk management

Greed blinds traders to risk. When you are focused on making big profits, it is easy to overlook how much you could lose if things go south. You might load up on risky trades without realising that, if the market turns, all your positions could hit their stop-loss levels at once — leading to massive losses.

To keep greed in check, you need good risk management tools. That means setting stop-loss orders and actually sticking to them. More importantly, before entering any trade, you should know the maximum amount you are willing to lose.

Regularly reviewing your positions and following a disciplined risk strategy ensures that greed does not push you into reckless trades. Staying within your risk limits protects your capital and keeps you from making emotional, high-stakes bets that could wipe out your gains.

4. Take regular breaks

Trading can feel overwhelming, especially when your expectations keep rising with your progress. It is easy to fall into the trap of always chasing the next big win, making it seem like you are never doing enough. That is why taking breaks and maintaining a healthy balance is crucial. Spend time on hobbies, connect with loved ones, and take care of your physical and mental well-being. These things help you reset, reflect, and return to trading with a fresh mindset. A balanced life also helps control emotions like greed.

Stepping away from the screens allows you to think clearly about your goals and avoid impulsive trades driven by the need for more. Set realistic goals, celebrate small wins, and remember — long-term trading success comes from a mix of discipline, learning, and self-care. Keeping this balance ensures you make rational decisions and continue growing steadily in the markets.

5. Turning greed into a positive force

While unchecked greed can be detrimental, the desire for more can also be harnessed in a positive way. Here are some ways to turn greed into a constructive force in your trading:

i. Channel ambition into continuous learning

Use your desire for success to fuel your commitment to continuous learning and improvement. Stay curious and seek out new knowledge, strategies, and insights to enhance your trading skills.

ii. Set higher standards for discipline

Let your ambition drive you to maintain high standards for discipline and consistency in your trading. Strive to execute your trading plan with precision and adhere to your risk management rules, even when tempted by potential profits.

CONCLUSION

In trading, greed is a powerful force that can drive both success and failure. By understanding the nature of greed and learning to manage it effectively, you can positively harness its energy and achieve long-term success. Remember, trading is not just about making money — it is about developing discipline, emotional intelligence, and a balanced approach to decision-making. By recognising and addressing the influence of greed in your trading, you can become a more resilient and successful trader, capable of navigating the markets with confidence and clarity.

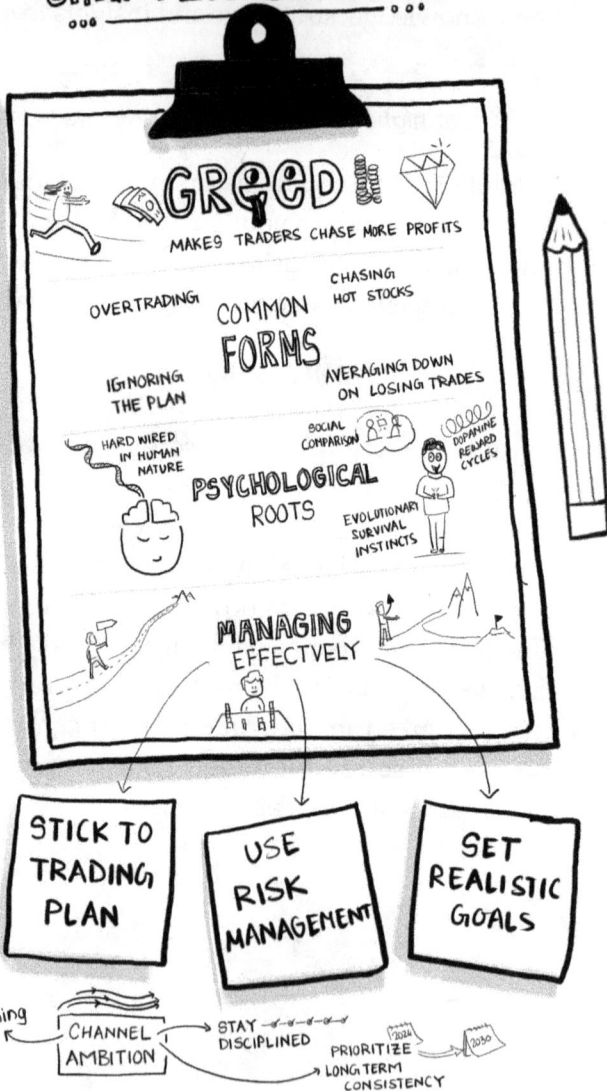

3

THE MINDSET OF A WINNER

"I always say you could publish rules in a newspaper and no one
would follow them. The key is consistency and discipline."
–Richard Dennis

Success in any field often comes down to having the right
mindset. This means being consistent, disciplined, and
thinking in non-traditional ways. One of the best thinkers on
this topic is Charlie Munger, a famous investor known for
his smart approach to solving problems and reaching goals.

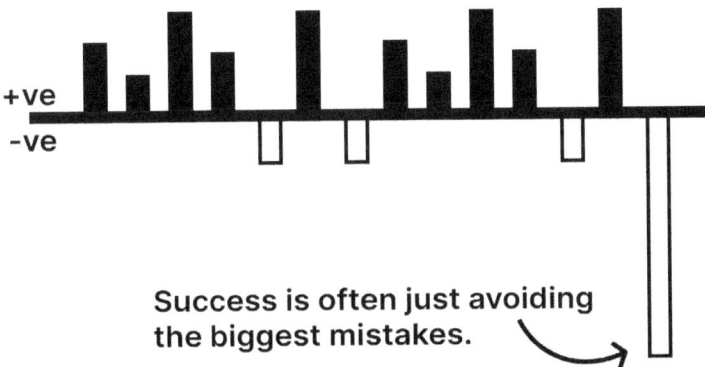

+ve
-ve

**Success is often just avoiding
the biggest mistakes.**

Munger teaches us to look at problems from the opposite perspective. Instead of asking, "How can I achieve success?" he suggests asking, "What can I do to fail?" By understanding what causes failure, we can avoid those mistakes and improve our chances of success.

Munger once said, "All I want to know is where I'm going to die so I'll never go there." This means that by knowing what leads to failure, we can stay away from it.

Similarly, to understand how to be a winner, we must first learn about the mindset of a loser and avoid making those errors.

Here are some characteristics of a trader with a loser mindset.

VICTIM MINDSET 101

- Blames the world for everything, never looks in the mirror.
- Believes life is unfair, but never questions his own choices.
- Sees obstacles as proof of bad luck, not challenges to overcome
- Thinks success is reserved for 'others,' not people like him.
- Waits for change but never takes the first step.
- Finds excuses faster than solutions.
- Sees himself as powerless, yet refuses to take control.

A VICTIM MINDSET: THE STORY OF MEERA

Meera was a hardworking and talented woman who had always dreamed of starting her own business. She had a great idea, put in endless hours, and invested all her savings to make it happen. But things did not go as planned. Customers were not coming, and expenses kept growing. She felt defeated. Every day, Meera sat in her empty store, feeling the weight of failure. Instead of looking at what she could improve, she blamed outside factors.

"The economy is bad."
"People don't understand my product."
"It's the competition's fault."

Meera focused on everything she could not control instead of what she could. She started believing that she had no power to change things. Her thoughts became negative:

"Why does this always happen to me?"
"No matter what I do, it never works."

As time passed, Meera lost motivation. She expected things to go wrong, and this mindset affected her actions. She stopped trying to market her business, thinking it would not help. She avoided networking because she believed no one could help her. Even when good opportunities came, she ignored them, convinced they would not work.

Her negativity also pushed people away. Meera often complained to friends and family, looking for sympathy instead of solutions. When they gave her advice, she dismissed it, saying it would not work for her. Eventually, people got tired of her negativity and stopped trying to help.

Every small problem reinforced her belief that she was meant to fail. A late shipment or a bad customer review felt like proof that nothing would ever work out. Instead of learning from these experiences, she used them as excuses to stay stuck. But in reality, Meera's biggest problem was not the market, the economy, or her competition—it was her own mindset. By blaming others and not accepting her own mistakes, she stopped learning and improving.

The victim mindset trapped her in a cycle of blame and inaction. She kept waiting for something to change externally, not realising that the real change had to come from within.

This is true for everyone, but especially for traders. Blaming the market, bad luck, or news reports is easy — but taking responsibility for your own actions is hard. The best traders focus on what they can control — their strategies, risk management, and emotional discipline. Instead of blaming external factors, they analyse their trades, find their mistakes, and learn from them. If you want to improve, stop looking for excuses and start looking within.

Lack of decision-making capability

One common problem among losing traders is doubt in their own decisions. This hesitation affects how they run their trading business. If you want to succeed, you must build confidence in your ability to make decisions.

Beginners often look to experts for advice on their trades. While learning from others is useful, relying too much on outside opinions weakens your confidence. If you

Confidence in trading is like an iceberg—what you see is just the tip; real mastery lies beneath.

always seek validation, you will struggle to trust your own judgment. The best approach is to learn from experts but base your trades on your own analysis.

Trading requires critical thinking to achieve exceptional results. You need to solve problems in your own way, instead of blindly following what works for others. The best traders I know do not just follow conventional wisdom—they understand their own system deeply and come up with their own solutions.

The truth is, most traders only have a surface-level understanding of what they are doing. They know the basics but have not truly explored the deeper mechanics of trading. This lack of depth is why many traders lack confidence and struggle with decision-making.

To build confidence, you need to question everything. Do not just accept strategies at face value—ask why they work, why the market moves a certain way, and how different factors interact. This habit of questioning leads to a deeper understanding, which in turn improves your ability to make smart, independent decisions.

The more you analyse and think critically, the more self-reliant and confident you will become in your trading.

Traders with a passive mindset believe that things will take care of themselves.

One common characteristic of a trader with a passive mindset is the belief that they have no control over the events affecting them. They think that if they are not performing well as a trader, it is not their fault. This mindset is detrimental to success. They believe that things will take care of themselves. While it is true that we do not have complete control over everything, and some things happen randomly, the majority of what happens to us is definitely under our control.

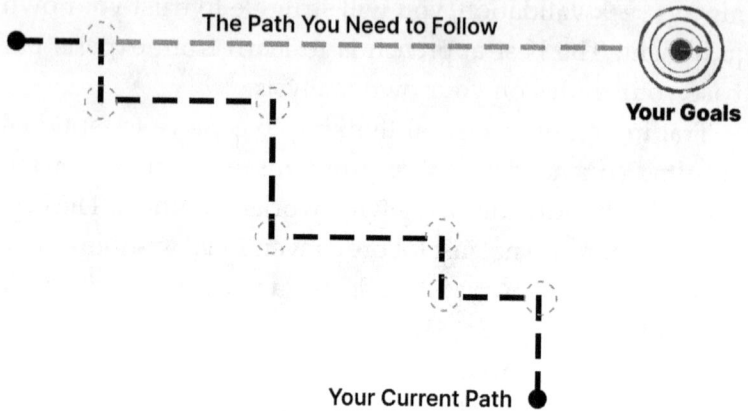

The Path You Need to Follow

Your Goals

Your Current Path

THE CONSEQUENCES OF A PASSIVE MINDSET

When traders believe that things will somehow work out on their own, they give up control over their results.

This passive mindset leads to several problems.

1. **Not being prepared:** Traders who think they have no control over their results often skip important steps like analysing the market, making a solid trading plan, or managing risk properly. Without preparation, they are more likely to struggle when the market moves unpredictably.

2. **Chasing the market instead of planning ahead:** Traders with this mindset wait for things to happen instead of preparing in advance. This leads to missed opportunities and poorly timed trades. Since they do not plan ahead, they react emotionally to short-term market moves, often making impulsive decisions instead of following a solid strategy.

3. **Blaming external factors:** Traders who think they have no control over their trading performance often blame external factors for their losses. This could be

market manipulation, economic events, or even bad luck. By externalising blame, they avoid introspection and fail to identify their own mistakes and areas for improvement.

4. **Unstable results and no real growth:** When traders do not take control of their actions, their performance becomes unpredictable. Wins feel like luck, and losses get blamed on external factors. This cycle leads to frustration and a lack of motivation, making it even harder to improve. Without accountability, they never truly learn from their mistakes or build the skills needed for long-term success.

5. **Dodging responsibility:** When traders assume that things will magically work out, they avoid owning up to their mistakes. They skip reviewing past trades, fail to learn from errors, and do not actively seek improvement. But responsibility is essential for growth — without it, they stay stuck in the same cycle, making the same mistakes over and over again.

ENTROPY: THE NATURAL DRIFT TOWARDS DISORDER

Weeds don't need permission to grow. Without effort, disorder takes over.

In physics, entropy explains how things naturally move toward disorder unless effort is made to maintain order.

Trading works the same way—if a trader does not actively manage their mindset and system, their performance will spiral into chaos and losses. A passive approach also creates emotional turmoil. When traders feel they have no control, their emotions swing wildly with market moves. This instability leads to random decisions, making trading even more unpredictable.

Like entropy breaking down systems over time, a trader's confidence and results degrade without conscious effort. Small mistakes pile up, losses add up, and setbacks grow larger—both financially and mentally. This losing mindset becomes a trap. The more a trader experiences disorder, the more they believe they have no control. That belief then reinforces their passive attitude, making their results even worse. It is a vicious cycle. Breaking free from this cycle takes a major shift in mindset and strategy. But many traders do not realise that they are stuck, so they keep repeating the same patterns, expecting different results.

WINNER MENTALITY

Now that we know a few key characteristics of a trader with a losing mindset, it is important to also understand the traits of a successful trader with a winning mentality. By recognising and adopting these positive characteristics, traders can shift their approach and improve their chances of success.

Traders with a winning mindset believe that mistakes are just opportunities to grow.

A trader with a winning mindset does not view mistakes as failures but as stepping stones to improvement. They understand that every misstep holds a lesson that can refine their strategy and sharpen their skills. Instead of ignoring their weaknesses, they actively seek them out, knowing that fixing small flaws early prevents bigger problems later.

Growth isn't about avoiding missteps, it's about using them to climb higher.

When setbacks happen, they do not get stuck in frustration. They analyse what went wrong, adjust their approach, and keep moving forward with even more clarity. By embracing mistakes, they build resilience and adaptability—two key traits of long-term success. They believe in the idea of "fail fast, learn faster," understanding that every mistake is a chance to improve. This mindset speeds up their learning curve, making them stronger traders over time. They also maintain a positive outlook. Rather than dwelling on losses, they focus on the lessons gained. They take full responsibility for their actions, knowing that accountability fuels progress. This approach keeps them sharp, adaptable, and ahead of the game in ever-changing market conditions.

THE GROWTH MINDSET

There are two types of mindsets that you can have as a trader—a growth mindset and a fixed mindset.

Growth Mindset

- Sees challenges as opportunities
- Learns from criticism
- Believes effort leads to improvement
- Embraces failure as part of growth

Fixed Mindset

- Avoids challenges
- Takes criticism personally
- Believes abilities are fixed
- Fears failure and avoids risks

Those with fixed mindsets believe that there are certain things they are not capable of doing at all, no matter how hard they work or how passionate they are about that particular thing. This belief limits their potential, as they often avoid challenges, give up easily, and see effort as fruitless.

Compared to this, those with a growth mindset believe that abilities and intelligence can be developed through dedication, hard work, and perseverance. They see challenges as opportunities to grow, embrace failure as a learning experience, and persist in the face of setbacks. This mindset helps develop a love for learning and resilience, which are required to achieve greatness.

I believe that if you try long enough you can grasp even the most complex things, and the best traders are often lifelong learners, they just never stop learning no matter how good they become at their craft. They believe that there is always something they can improve in their system to get even better results.

Someone with a fixed mindset will put a limit to how much they can achieve in terms of their account growth or even something like the number of hours they can put into researching and building a new strategy. They stop themselves from being in situations where they could potentially gain a lot—thus missing out on those positive outlier situations, which could give a big boost to their overall profitability.

Traders with a winning mindset do exactly the opposite. They recognise that there is no ceiling to their potential and continuously push their boundaries. In essence, the winning mindset in trading is characterised by a constant pursuit of improvement and an openness to learning and adapting.

Traders with a winning mindset are not afraid to change their mind.

Markets are always shifting, influenced by countless factors. A winning trader knows that sticking to outdated ideas or rigid strategies can be dangerous. Instead of resisting change, they embrace it, adapting their approach whenever new evidence suggests a better path.

You can't change the direction of the wind, but you can adjust your sails.

Most people fear change—it is human nature to cling to what feels familiar, even when it is no longer useful. In trading, this fear can be costly. Many traders hold on to old strategies, hoping they will work again, even when the market has clearly moved on.

Winning traders, however, see change as an opportunity, not a threat. They constantly reassess their strategies, making adjustments based on what is actually working now, not what worked in the past. Their mindset is built on logic, not ego. When new information challenges their beliefs, they do not take it personally. Instead, they see it as valuable feedback — another chance to refine their approach and get better.

HOW TO DEVELOP A WINNER'S MENTALITY

Now that we have discussed the key traits of a trader with a winning mindset, it is essential to understand how you can cultivate the same mindset for yourself. Here are some ideas and exercises to help you shift from a losing mindset to a winning one:

1. Daily affirmations: Reinforcing principles for a winning mindset

Science backs the power of affirmations. Studies show they can boost confidence, enhance problem-solving under stress, and strengthen goal-oriented thinking. Research in the journal *Social Cognitive and Affective Neuroscience* found that self-affirmation activates the brain's reward centres — areas linked to self-worth and motivation. Another study in *Psychological Science* revealed that people who practised affirmations performed better under pressure.

Why do affirmations work? Because they reshape the way you think. They help shift your focus from doubts and fears to possibilities and strengths. Over time, this rewiring influences your decisions, actions, and overall approach to challenges. For traders, affirmations can reinforce discipline, patience, and resilience. Here are a few examples:

- I make decisions based on logic and data, not emotions.
- I am disciplined and patient in my trading strategy.

- Every mistake is an opportunity to grow.
- The best days often come after the worst days. Stay patient and vigilant.

By repeating affirmations daily, you train your mind to adopt the mindset of a successful trader. This is not just positive thinking — it is mental conditioning that strengthens your ability to stay focused, make sound decisions, and keep pushing forward.

2. Visualisation

Success begins in the mind. See yourself winning before the world does.

Visualisation, or mental rehearsal, is the practice of imagining yourself achieving a goal or performing a task successfully. It involves picturing every detail — what you see, hear, and feel in that moment. This technique is widely used in sports, performance coaching, therapy, and personal development to enhance focus and confidence. The concept is not new. Ancient cultures used visualisation in meditation and spiritual practices. But in the 1960s and 1970s, psychologists began systematically applying it to performance improvement. One of the key figures in this field was Dr. Maxwell Maltz, a plastic surgeon turned psychologist. In his book *Psycho-Cybernetics* (1960), he introduced mental imagery as a tool for improving self-image and achieving success. Maltz observed that the brain struggles to distinguish between real and imagined experiences, meaning that visualising success can actually help create it. For traders, this insight is powerful. If you can mentally rehearse executing trades with confidence, managing risk, and staying disciplined, your brain will treat these imagined experiences as real. Over time, this practice strengthens your ability to stay composed and make smart decisions under pressure. To take full advantage of this activity incorporate it into your daily routines and perform it consistently. Here are some key principles to keep in mind when performing visualisation for your trading:

Step 1: Visualise in as much detail as possible, using all senses to create a realistic mental image.

Step 2: Practise visualisation regularly to reinforce mental patterns and create a habit of positive mental rehearsal.

Step 3: Connect emotionally with the imagined scenario to enhance motivation and commitment.

Step 4: Visualise success and focus on achieving desired outcomes rather than dwelling on potential difficulties.

   Incorporating all of these key principles in your visualising routine will help you build a winning mindset.

3. Building confidence and self-belief

Kobe Bryant once said, "Confidence comes from preparation. When the game is on the line, I'm not asking myself to do something I haven't done thousands of times before."

Confidence is not something you magically wake up with one day—it is built through repetition and preparation. Your subconscious mind needs proof that you are capable, and the best way to provide that proof is through consistent practise and experience. One of the most effective ways to do this in trading is by creating a playbook—a detailed record of your strategy's past trades. This playbook should include how you planned, entered, and managed those trades, along with their outcomes. By regularly reviewing and analysing your past performance, you start spotting patterns, refining your strategy, and gaining trust in your own decision-making. Over time, this process reinforces your understanding of the market and makes you more decisive. When you step into a live trade, you are not second-guessing—you have already seen and prepared for similar situations before. Just as Kobe Bryant spent hours perfecting his shot so he could execute effortlessly under pressure, traders can use their playbook to develop a mindset rooted in preparation and experience.

4. Remember your wins

Sometimes, shifting from a negative mindset to a positive one is as simple as reminding yourself of your past wins. It is not a magic fix, but it helps you zoom out and view your trading journey from a long term perspective instead of getting caught up in short-term ups and downs.

Trading is full of randomness—some things are simply out of your control. If you judge yourself based only on short-term results, you will either get too excited when things go well or too discouraged when they do not. By revisiting your past wins, you remind yourself that you *can* succeed and that your strategies *do* work over time. Keeping a journal of your best trades—along with the decisions and strategies that led to them—can be a powerful tool. When you hit a rough patch, looking back at this journal can boost your confidence and help you stay committed to your plan. The goal is not to ignore mistakes but to balance them with proof that you are capable. This practice keeps your emotions in check and reinforces the mindset needed for long-term success.

5. Reward efforts, not outcomes

✔ How a Pro Trader thinks

- Good Trade = Followed the Plan, Managed Risk
- Bad Trade = Broke Rules, Poor Execution

✖ How a Retail Trader thinks

- Green PNL = Good Trade
- Red PNL = Bad Trade

It is natural to label your wins as "good trades" and your losses as "bad trades" if you are only looking at your profit and loss. But is that really what matters? The truth is, profit and loss is influenced by many factors outside your control—market conditions, random fluctuations, even pure luck. What *is* fully within your control? Your *process*.

A winning trader does not measure success just by profit and loss. Instead, they focus on how well they executed their strategy, how disciplined they were, and whether they followed their rules.

When you start rewarding yourself for sticking to your process — not just for making money — you reinforce the habits that lead to long-term success. This shift in focus keeps your mindset stable, no matter what the market throws at you. Instead of getting caught up in short-term results, you build confidence in your ability to trade well over time. Celebrate the right things: executing your strategy, maintaining discipline, and learning from each trade. When you prioritise the process, the profits take care of themselves.

6. Control the controllable

Things you can't control

Short Term PNL

Market Direction

News & Events

- Entry & Exit Strategies
- Risk Management
- Position Sizing

Things you can control

Many traders feel disappointed — not just because they are not hitting their goals, but because their trading is not unfolding the way they expected it to. They anticipate a strong winning streak but hit a rough patch instead. Then, just when they feel like giving up, things unexpectedly improve. This unpredictability creates frustration, making it seem like they have no control over their results.

But here is the flaw in that thinking: traders often focus on things they *cannot* control — market movements, random fluctuations, and short-term outcomes. The more they obsess over these external factors, the more powerless they feel. The real key to a winning mindset is shifting focus to what *is* within your control:

Entries and trailing mechanisms – Following a well-defined strategy instead of chasing trades on impulse.

Risk management – Setting stop-losses and managing downside risk so no single trade can knock you out.

Position sizing – Allocating capital wisely to balance risk and maximise returns over time.

When traders master these elements, they stop feeling like victims of the market and start playing a game they can actually win. The goal is not to predict every move—it is to *control your approach* so that, over time, the edge works in your favour.

On the other hand, traders often fixate on elements outside their control, which may lead to undue stress and dissatisfaction. These include:

- **Market direction:** You cannot predict or control the overall direction of the market. Trying to anticipate every market move can lead to frustration and poor decision-making.
- **Profit and loss targets:** Setting rigid profit targets for a month can be counterproductive. Market conditions vary, and focusing solely on financial outcomes can detract from the disciplined execution of a trading plan.

- **Market reactions:** External events and market news can significantly impact market movements, and these are beyond any trader's control.

By concentrating on the controllable aspects of trading, such as entries, exits, risk management, and position sizing, traders can develop a more disciplined and consistent approach. This shift in focus reduces frustration and enhances the likelihood of sustainable success. Recognising that you cannot control the market, but you can control your response to it, is key to building a winning trading mindset.

7. Start trusting yourself

Every small promise you keep is a step up the trust ladder. The higher you climb, the stronger your confidence.

One defining trait of successful traders is their unshakable self-trust. This trust is not just about believing in their trading system—it runs deeper. It comes from a solid inner confidence, built through their actions, habits, and the way they live their life. To develop this self-trust, traders need to be true to themselves and consistently follow through on their commitments. Stephen Covey, in *The 7 Habits of Highly Effective People*, highlights this principle: keeping promises to yourself builds personal integrity, which in turn strengthens self-trust. In trading, this means:

1. Sticking to your trading plan, even when emotions tempt you to stray.
2. Honouring your stop-losses and position sizing rules, no matter what.
3. Taking full responsibility for your results instead of blaming the market.

When you consistently do what you say you will do, your confidence grows. You stop second-guessing yourself, and decision-making becomes more fluid. Over time, this trust in yourself becomes one of your greatest trading edges. When you honour your commitments in all areas of life, you build a sense of reliability and trustworthiness within yourself. This can include small daily promises, such as getting up at a specific time, exercising regularly, or dedicating time to personal development. Each action, no matter how small, reinforces your belief in your ability to follow through. For example, if you commit to waking up at 6 a.m. every day and you consistently do it, you start to trust yourself more. This habit of self-discipline then translates to your trading activities. When you promise yourself to stick to your trading plan, manage your risk, or take breaks at specific times, you are more likely to follow through because you have built a strong foundation of self-trust.

By consistently doing what you say you will do, you develop a habit of integrity and reliability that permeates all aspects of your life. This approach to self-trust enhances your ability to remain disciplined and make confident decisions, even in the face of uncertainty.

CHAPTER SUMMARY

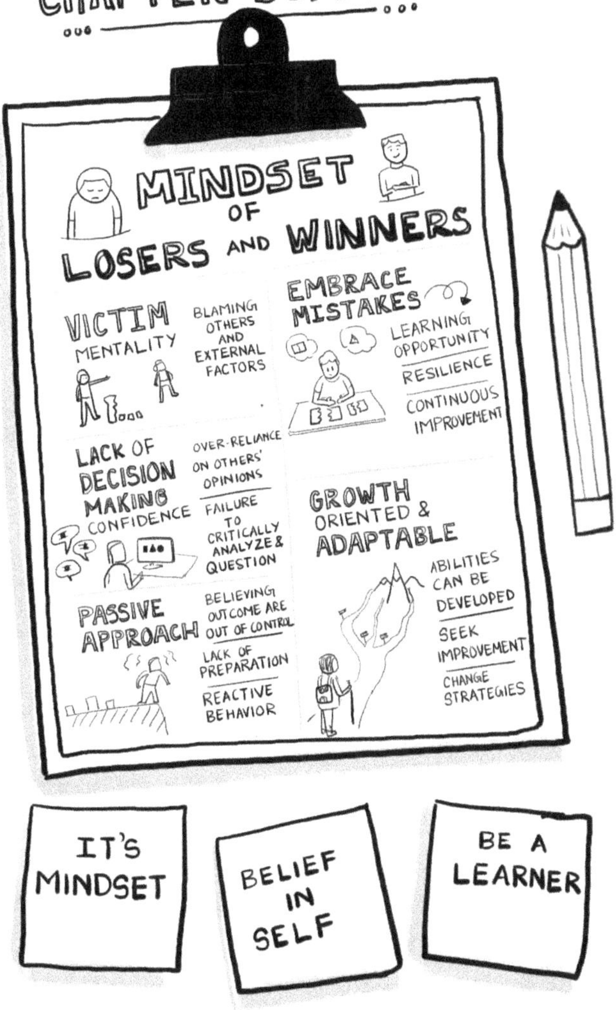

4

UNDERSTANDING COGNITIVE BIASES IN TRADING

"The greatest deception we face is not from the world around us, but from the mind within us."

In the last few chapters, we talked a lot about the emotional side of trading—how fear, greed, and the mindset of a winner can shape our decisions. But there is another important factor we need to look at—cognitive biases. These are mental shortcuts our brains take, often without us realising it, and they can mess with our decision-making. We like to think we are logical and rational, that we make decisions based on facts and reasoning. After all, humans are the only species that can think critically, analyse complex situations, and make choices beyond just instinct. But time and again, we make decisions that do not really make sense—choices influenced by false beliefs, flawed thinking and emotions.

And it is not just individual traders who fall into this trap. History is full of examples where cognitive biases led to huge failures.

Take the 2008 financial crisis, for example.

It was not just about bad loans or risky investments —
cognitive biases played a big role. People followed the
crowd, believing housing prices would keep rising forever
(that is herd mentality). Banks and investors stuck to old
valuations instead of accepting new data (that is anchoring
bias). And many traders were overly confident, thinking
they could predict the market better than they actually
could. The result? A global meltdown that affected millions
of lives. These biases do not just cause small problems; they
can shake entire markets.

2008 GLOBAL FINANCIAL CRISIS

If we want to be better traders, we need to recognise these
biases and deal with them. Ignoring them is not just a missed
opportunity — it can lead to major losses. In this chapter, we
will go over the most common cognitive biases in trading.
We will break them down in a simple way — what they are,
why they happen, and most importantly, how you can spot
and avoid them. By understanding these biases, you will be
able to make better decisions and trade with more clarity
and confidence. So, let us dive in and uncover the hidden
forces that may be influencing your trades without you even
realising it. The more aware we are, the better we can protect

ourselves from the mistakes that have taken down even the biggest players in the financial world.

1. Survivorship bias

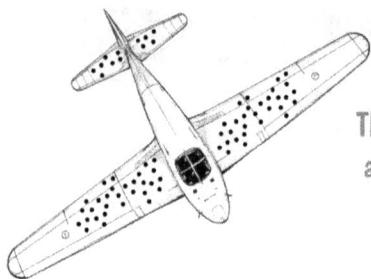

The stories you don't hear are just as important as the ones you do.

We have all heard stories of people who went on to achieve incredible things — entrepreneurs who built massive businesses from nothing, athletes who defied the odds, and traders who turned small accounts into fortunes. These stories are inspiring, no doubt. But they also create a misleading picture of success. We celebrate the winners, but what about the countless others who tried and failed? Their stories rarely get told, leaving us with a one-sided view of what it really takes to succeed. This is called survivorship bias. It is when we focus only on the success stories and ignore the failures, even though the failures can teach us just as much — if not more. Think about it — how often do you hear about the startups that did not make it? Or the traders who lost everything trying to copy someone they admired? These stories are not as exciting, but they are crucial for understanding the real risks involved.

One of the best examples of survivorship bias comes from World War II. The military wanted to reinforce fighter planes, so they studied the ones that made it back and added armour to the areas with the most bullet holes. But a statistician, Abraham Wald, pointed out a flaw in this thinking. The planes they studied were the survivors. The ones that got hit in other areas never made it back. The real weak spots were the ones they were not seeing. By focusing only on the survivors, they almost missed the most important lesson. Survivorship bias works the same way in trading. We hear about traders who took big risks and made millions. These are the stories that get turned into books and movies. But for every one of those, there are countless others who took the same risks and lost everything. The difference? Often, it is not skill or strategy—it is just luck.

When we fall for survivorship bias, we start ignoring the real risks. We see the traders who made it big and think, "That could be me!" So we chase high-risk trades, believing we will be the next success story, without realising how rare those outcomes actually are. The reality is, most people who take those risks do not make it. That is why it is smarter to focus on managing risk rather than chasing fast money.

As the saying goes, *"There are old traders and there are bold traders, but there are no old and bold traders."* The ones who last in this game are not the ones taking reckless bets—they are the ones who manage their risks and avoid blowing up their accounts. Survivorship bias is dangerous because it plays on our natural desire to succeed. We want to believe we can be like the people we admire. But if we want to make smart trading decisions, we have to remember: for every success story, there are many untold stories of failure. By learning from both the winners *and* the losers, we can build a realistic, sustainable approach to trading—one that is not based on wishful thinking, but on solid, long-term strategy.

2. Pattern recognition or illusion?

The mind craves patterns, even in the chaos. But not everything that looks connected is real.

We have a natural habit of looking for patterns in almost everything. It is wired into us, probably because, throughout history, spotting patterns helped us survive. Think about it—if our ancestors noticed that dark clouds often meant a storm was coming, they could find shelter before the rain hit. This ability to recognise patterns helped them predict what might happen next and stay safe. But this instinct is not always helpful, especially when we start seeing patterns where none actually exist. This is called the *clustering illusion*—our brain's tendency to find meaning in random events. That is why we see faces in clouds, believe in lucky streaks, or think a completely random sequence has some deeper significance.

In trading, this habit can be dangerous. Imagine a trader who notices that a stock seems to go up every time a certain news event happens. He starts believing that there is a connection, even if it is just a coincidence. Convinced that he has found a hidden market signal, he starts making trades based on it. But in reality, there is no real pattern—just randomness. This kind of thinking can lead to overconfidence. You start believing you have cracked the code, that you have found a "sure thing." But when the market moves unpredictably—as it always does—you are caught off guard. The key is to remind yourself that not every pattern in the market means something. Understanding this will keep you grounded and help you avoid falling into the clustering illusion trap. In trading, it is not about finding patterns everywhere—it is about knowing which ones actually matter.

3. Resulting bias

```
                  ┌──────────────────┐
                  │ Sell Stock Early │
                  └──────────────────┘
                           │
           ┌───────────────┴───────────────┐
           ▼                               ▼
  ┌──────────────┐              ┌──────────────┐
  │ Stock Soars  │              │ Stock Crashes│
  └──────────────┘              └──────────────┘
           │                               │
           └───────────────┬───────────────┘
                           │
           ┌───────────────────────────────┐
           │ Was the Decision Good or Bad?  │
           └───────────────────────────────┘
```

Resulting bias is tricky because it makes us believe that a decision's quality depends entirely on how things turn out. But in trading, where luck and randomness play a big role, that is not always true. Let us break it down. Looking back, it is easy to see a winning trade and think, "That was a great decision!" or a losing trade and think, "That was a terrible call." But the truth is, a good decision can still lead to a bad outcome, and sometimes a bad decision works out just by luck. That is resulting bias in action. For example, imagine you sell a stock after making a nice profit, but the next day, it shoots up even higher. You might feel like you made a mistake. But what if the stock had crashed instead? You would be glad you sold when you did. The decision itself was not good or bad—it is just that the outcome made you feel a certain way about it.

Now, why does this matter for traders? If you judge your trades only by their results, you might start doubting your strategy.

A few losing trades could make you think your approach is wrong, even if it is actually solid. This can lead to constantly changing strategies, making your results even more unpredictable. The key to avoiding resulting bias is to focus on the *process*, not just the outcome. Judge your trades based on whether you followed your strategy, not whether you made or lost money.

When you stick to a solid plan and stay consistent, you avoid the emotional rollercoaster that comes from obsessing over short-term results. In the end, it is not about winning every trade—it is about staying on track for the long run.

4. Coincidence

The other day, my friend Vaibhav, an experienced trader, messaged me, clearly frustrated. "I just sold this stock I was holding for days. It wasn't moving at all. But the moment I sold it, it shot up! It's like someone is watching my trades and messing with me!"

If you have been trading for a while, you have probably felt the same way at some point. It almost seems like the market is playing tricks on you—waiting for you to exit before taking off. But in reality, this is just a coincidence. Vaibhav's experience is not unique. Many traders believe that some invisible force—market operators, big players, or even luck—is working against them. But the truth is, the market is not out to get anyone. Stocks move for countless reasons, and sometimes, it just *happens* that they go up right after you sell. The problem starts when traders like Vaibhav try to make sense of these random events by blaming external factors instead of looking at their own decisions. If you convince yourself that the market is rigged against you, you stop focusing on what *you* can improve—like your strategy, patience, or timing.

Vaibhav could have asked himself: *Did I sell too soon? Was I expecting instant results instead of following my system?* Instead, he fell into the trap of blaming the market. And that is dangerous because it shifts the focus away from what really matters—your own trading decisions. The key to avoiding this mindset is to accept that coincidences will happen. The market is chaotic, full of random movements, and not everything needs a deeper explanation. The sooner traders accept this, the sooner they stop making emotional, fear-driven decisions. If Vaibhav wants to be a consistently profitable trader, he needs to realise that the market is not against him—it is just doing what it always does. The only thing he can control is *how he reacts*. And that is where real progress begins.

5. Gambler's Fallacy

The gambler's fallacy is a common mistake where people believe that if something keeps happening, it is less likely to continue—or if it has not happened in a while, it is "due" to happen soon. Take a coin flip, for example. If you flip a coin three times and it lands on heads each time, you might feel like the next flip *has* to be tails. But that is not true. The odds are still 50-50, just like before. Each flip is independent of the last one. This kind of thinking can be dangerous in trading. Let us say you have had several losing trades in a row. You might start believing that a winning trade is "due" and take bigger risks, expecting the market to finally turn in your favour. But just like the coin toss, every trade has its own probabilities. What happened before does not change the odds of what happens next. Take Akshay, for example. After a streak of losing trades, he was convinced that a win was around the corner. So he started increasing his position sizes, thinking he would make back his losses faster. But the losses kept coming, and before he knew it, his account was wiped out. This is the gambler's fallacy in action — believing that the market would "correct" itself in his favour, Akshay took unnecessary risks and paid the price.

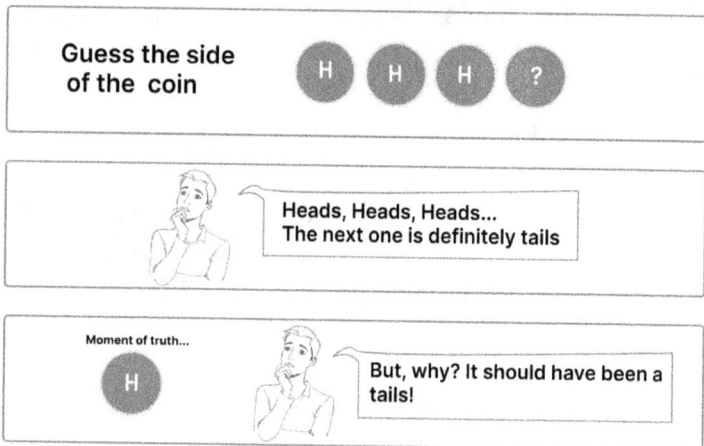

Guess the side of the coin
H   H   H   ?

Heads, Heads, Heads...
The next one is definitely tails

Moment of truth...
H
But, why? It should have been a tails!

One of the most famous examples of this fallacy happened in 1913 at the Monte Carlo Casino. The roulette ball landed on black multiple times in a row, and gamblers started piling money on red, believing that black *couldn't* keep coming up. But they were wrong. The ball landed on black 26 times in a row, and they lost millions. The key takeaway? The market does not "remember" what happened before, and it does not "owe" you anything. Each trade is independent, and the best way to succeed is to stick to logic, strategy, and risk management—*not* superstitions.

6. Loss aversion

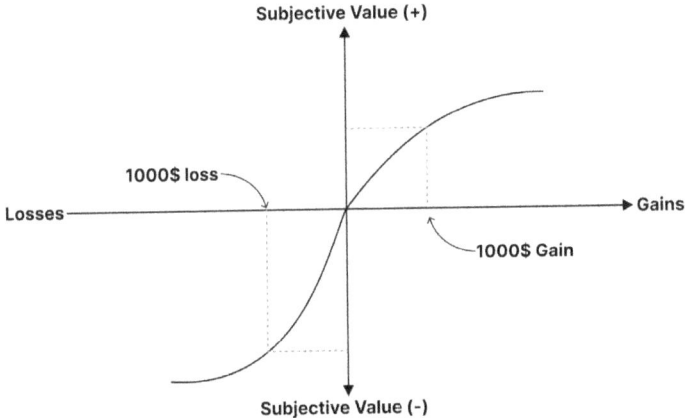

Loss aversion seems simple at first—it is the idea that losses feel worse than equivalent gains feel good. But in trading, it runs much deeper, shaping decisions in ways we do not always realise. Studies show that the pain of losing is about twice as intense as the joy of winning. That is why traders often hold on to losing trades, hoping they will bounce back, while cutting winning trades short to "lock in" profits.

Let us say you are in a trade that is showing a solid profit. You know it might have more room to run, but the thought of giving back those gains feels unbearable. So, you sell early. That is loss aversion in action—the fear of losing what you *already* have outweighs the potential reward of holding.

Now flip the situation. You are in a losing trade, and instead of cutting it, you tell yourself, *"It'll turn around. If I don't sell, I haven't really lost anything."* But avoiding the pain of taking a loss does not make the loss go away. If anything, small losses can snowball into devastating ones. This bias is not just a trading flaw — it is evolutionary. Our ancestors needed to be hypersensitive to losses because survival depended on it. Finding food was great, but eating something poisonous? That could be fatal. So our brains evolved to weigh losses more heavily than gains. Helpful for survival, not so much for trading. This is why traders make irrational decisions. We *know* we should cut losers and let winners run, yet we do the opposite. The good news? Awareness is the first step to fixing it. A structured trading plan with clear rules for cutting losses and taking profits can help remove emotions from decision-making. Another tactic is shifting perspective — stop obsessing over individual trades and focus on long-term performance. Small losses are not failures; they are just part of the process. Loss aversion is a powerful force, but it does not have to control you. Recognise it, manage it, and you will make better trading decisions — ones based on strategy, not fear.

7. The house money effect

The house money effect is a sneaky little trap that catches even experienced traders. It is that feeling you get after a big win — where the profits in your account suddenly feel like "free money." You start thinking, *"I can afford to take a bigger risk now because even if I lose, I'm still ahead."* But that is exactly where the danger begins.

Say you just made a solid 10,000 profit on your 1,00,000 trading account. Your balance is now 1,10,000, but instead of treating it as your new base, you mentally separate that 10,000 as "extra." It feels like a bonus — money you can afford to gamble with. That is the house money effect in action. You start taking bigger risks, thinking, *"Even if I lose this,*

I'll be back where I started." But here is the reality: that 10,000 is just as much yours as the original 1,00,000. Once it is in your account, it deserves the same level of discipline and risk management.

The real problem? Once you start treating money differently, your decision-making shifts. Maybe you chase setups you would not normally take or size up beyond what is reasonable. And when that "extra" 10,000 disappears, frustration kicks in. Now you are digging into your original 100,000, trying to make it back — and that is how a small lapse in discipline can spiral into significant losses.

The best way to avoid this? See every rupee in your account as equal. A profit is not "house money" — it is *your* money. Stay disciplined, respect your capital, and do not let a winning streak lure you into reckless decisions. So how do you avoid falling into this trap?

1. **Treat all your money equally:** Once that profit is in your account, it is no different from the rest of your capital. Do not mentally separate it as "play money." It is yours, and it deserves the same respect and careful management as the rest.

2. **Stay disciplined after a win**: Winning trades can give you a boost of confidence, but do not let that lead to reckless behaviour. Stick to your plan, and do not increase your risk just because you are on a hot streak. Remember, consistency is key in trading, not the occasional big win.

The house money effect is all about mindset. By recognising that every rupee in your account is equally valuable, you can avoid the temptation to gamble with your profits and keep your trading strategy on a steady, disciplined path.

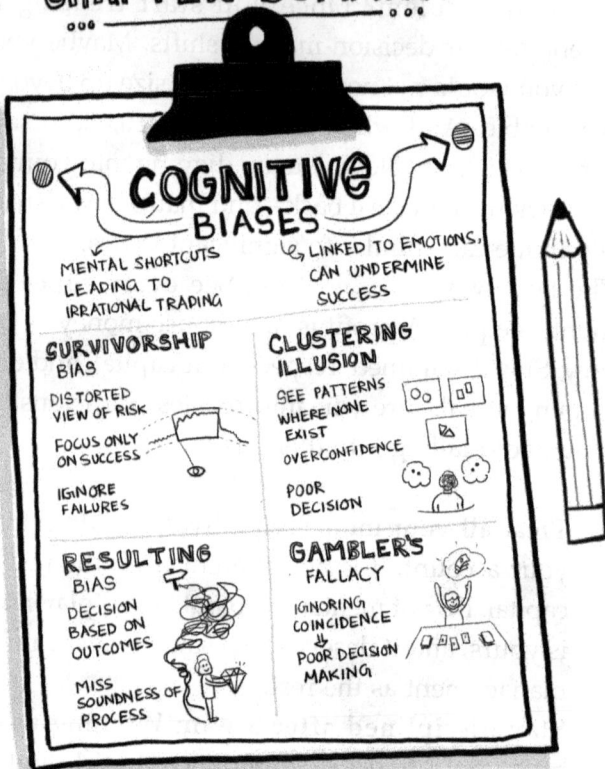

SECTION II

DEVELOPING A GOOD TRADING PROCESS

"Excellence is not an act, but a habit."
— Aristotle

In this section, we shift focus to the development of a trading process that is aligned with your unique personality and strengths. Building a successful trading process is not just about following a set of rules; it is about finding a rhythm that works for you.

We will explore how to create a system that feels natural and sustainable, allowing you to trade with confidence and consistency. You will discover the importance of flexibility and how thinking outside the box can give you an edge in the markets. This section is all about establishing a solid foundation that will support your growth as a trader.

5

FINDING THE RIGHT TRADING SYSTEM FOR YOU

"Knowing yourself is the beginning of all wisdom."
—Aristotle

We humans are peculiar creatures—so alike, yet so different. Like branches of a massive tree, we grow in similar ways, yet each takes its own direction, finding a unique place in the world. This individuality is what makes us special. As a trader, understanding this is very important. Often, what we see as weaknesses are actually strengths in disguise—traits that might seem unusual to others but are second nature to us.

And what comes naturally to us? That is our superpower. The problem is, most people ignore their own superpowers. Instead, they chase after the strengths of others—usually those of more successful traders. But in doing so, they turn themselves into copies. And a copy is never as good as the original. That is just how it is. This does not just hurt performance; it messes with your mind. You become someone you are not, which leads to frustration and self-doubt. It is a cycle that keeps pulling you further away from where you should be. Yet, most people do not stop to break free from it.

This might sound a bit philosophical — and in some ways, it is. But to truly understand trading, you first need to understand *yourself*. Once you do that, everything else starts falling into place.

THE IMPORTANCE OF BUILDING A SYSTEM THAT ALIGNS WITH YOUR CORE BELIEFS

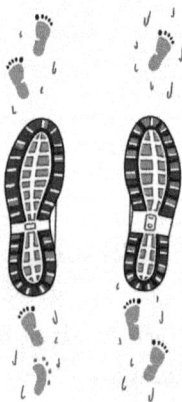

The footprints you follow should be your own. A trading system that doesn't fit you will always feel like someone else's shoes, uncomfortable and unsustainable.

As a trader, your goal should be to build a system that aligns with your core beliefs about the market. If your system does not match how you see the market, sticking to it will feel like a constant battle. For example, if you believe in fundamental analysis but try to force yourself into a purely technical trading approach, you will struggle. It will not feel natural, and sooner or later, you will find yourself second-guessing every move. Simply put, your beliefs and your trading system need to be in sync.

Here is another way to look at it: Say you are naturally cautious, but you try to adopt a high-risk, high-reward strategy. You will likely experience stress and hesitation, which can lead to poor execution and underperformance. On the flip side, if you are comfortable taking risks but force yourself into a conservative trading approach, you might get bored and start overtrading just to feel engaged. This misalignment is one of the biggest reasons traders struggle. The best traders understand their strengths and weaknesses and build their systems accordingly. They do not try to be someone they are not. Instead, they play to their natural tendencies, which allows them to trade with confidence and consistency.

So, take a step back and reflect. Are you a trend follower or a contrarian? Do you prefer short-term trades or long-term investments? Do you like structured rules, or do you thrive with more flexibility?

Understanding these aspects of yourself will help you create a system that feels natural and sustainable — one that leads to better performance and less stress. At the end of the day, in trading (just like in life), staying true to yourself is key. Embrace your uniqueness, and let it guide you to success.

Not everything you are inclined towards will be profitable

One key thing to remember when building a trading system is that not everything you are naturally drawn to will be profitable. Some traits, no matter how ingrained, will almost always lead to negative results over time. That is why finding the right balance is crucial — your system should align with your natural tendencies, but it also needs to be grounded in fundamental market principles. If you build a system solely based on what feels comfortable while ignoring how the market actually works, you are setting yourself up for failure.

For example, the market rewards patience and discipline. If you are naturally impatient, you might feel the urge to jump into trades too quickly, leading to impulsive decisions and unnecessary losses. On the flip side, if you are overly cautious, you might hesitate too much and miss out on great opportunities. A well-structured system helps neutralise these tendencies. By setting clear, mechanical rules for entries and exits, you remove emotion from the equation, ensuring that your decisions are not driven purely by impulse or fear.

Beyond your personal traits, it is just as important to understand market tendencies. The market moves in cycles—trends, consolidations, reversals. Recognising these patterns allows you to build a system that aligns not just with your personality but also with the way the market actually behaves. When you strike the right balance between your natural tendencies and market realities, you create a trading system that is both comfortable to follow and effective in the long run.

Not everything that is profitable needs to be tackled head-on: find your own niche

When I started trading, I had this idea that I would focus on one setup, master it completely, and trade it to its full potential. But as I learned more, I realised just how many different styles and strategies existed. It was exciting, and I started exploring setups from other traders as well as my own observations. I thought adding more setups would improve my results. Instead, I ended up overwhelmed. One strategy would signal a buy, while another would suggest waiting. The more setups I tried, the more confused I became.

Natural tendencies   **Market Realities**

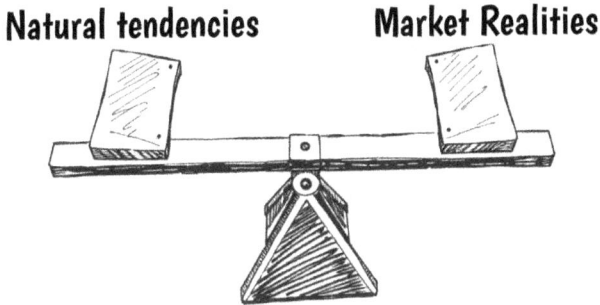

Instead of improving, I found myself second-guessing every move. The problem was not with the new strategies—they worked for others. The problem was with me. I was not ready to handle so many different approaches at once. My performance did improve, but very slowly. If I had focused on mastering one setup first, I could have progressed much faster. This led to an important realisation: I needed to commit to one thing at a time. Once I became consistent with a setup, I could gradually explore new strategies. This shift made a huge difference. My trading improved, my stress levels dropped, and I started enjoying the process more. Looking back, I wondered why I had not done this sooner.

Many traders fall into the same trap. They believe that mastering multiple setups will make them more successful. But in reality, trying to trade everything at once often leads to confusion, frustration, and inconsistency. Finding your niche means identifying what works best for you and sticking to it. Focus on your strengths, build confidence, and develop consistency. Once you have mastered one setup, you can slowly expand your trading toolkit.

In trading, less is often more. Instead of chasing multiple strategies, focus on quality over quantity. Master a few setups, and your results and peace of mind, will improve.

THE IMPORTANCE OF PIVOTING AS A TRADER (KNOW WHEN TO CHANGE STYLES, MAKE BIG CHANGES)

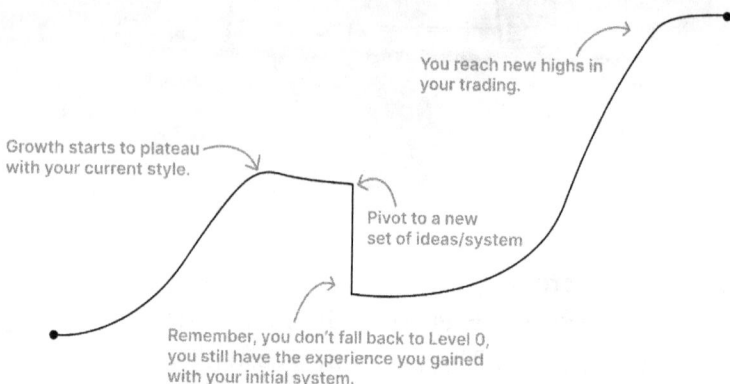

You reach new highs in
your trading.

Growth starts to plateau
with your current style.

Pivot to a new
set of ideas/system

Remember, you don't fall back to Level 0,
you still have the experience you gained
with your initial system.

Now that we have covered the problem of spreading yourself too thin, let us talk about when it makes sense to explore new strategies or even change your trading system entirely. Pivoting is a skill not everyone has. It takes humility to step away from something familiar and patience to learn something new. Most people avoid change — even when their current approach is not working — because the unknown feels risky. It is easier to stick with old habits, even if they are holding you back, than to adopt new ones that might lead to success. But here is the reality: if you always do what you have always done, you will always get what you have always got. That does not mean you should overhaul your system just because you are having a rough patch. Instead, focus on your overall trajectory. Are you improving over time? There are multiple ways to measure this. Your profit and loss (P&L) is the obvious one, but other factors matter too — like peace of mind, ease of execution, and consistency. If your results are improving, then your system is working. But if your performance is flat or declining despite going through market conditions that should have been favourable to your strategy, then it is time to pivot. For example, if your system performs well in trending markets but struggles in range-bound conditions, you might need to refine your approach or learn strategies that work better in choppy environments.

Sometimes, small tweaks — like adjusting your risk management or fine-tuning your entry and exit rules — can make a big difference. Remember, pivoting does not mean throwing away everything you have learned. It is about evolving, not starting over. You are integrating new ideas with what already works to build a stronger, more adaptable system. So take a step back and assess your trading journey. Are you progressing? Are you adjusting to market changes? If not, do not be afraid to pivot. The worst thing you can do is stay stuck in a cycle that is not working.

THE CHOICE BETWEEN PROFITABILITY AND MENTAL PEACE

One thing you realise after years in this industry is that every trader faces a choice: chase higher profits or aim for peace of mind. Some traders go all in for maximum profit. They push themselves hard, taking on stress to squeeze every last bit out of the markets. It can lead to big returns, but it also comes with mental strain and pressure. Then there are traders who focus on peace of mind. They could take bigger risks for higher profits, but they choose not to. Their goal is to make enough money without unnecessary stress. For them, trading is about balance—staying calm and focused while still being profitable. This choice is personal, and there is no right or wrong answer. Do not let anyone tell you which path you should take because everyone's situation is different. What works for one trader might not work for another. For example, if you are young with fewer responsibilities, you might be comfortable taking on more risk and stress to chase bigger profits. But if you have a family or other obligations, you may prefer a steadier approach that prioritises stability. The key is to be honest with yourself.

Do you thrive under pressure, or do you prefer a more relaxed pace? Are you looking for fast gains, or do you want consistent, long-term growth? The best traders figure out what works for them. They understand that trading is a marathon, not a sprint. Keeping their mental capital intact is just as important as managing their financial capital.

So, whether you choose to maximise profits or focus on peace of mind, make sure it aligns with your goals and overall well-being. That is what will keep you in the game for the long run.

CHAPTER SUMMARY

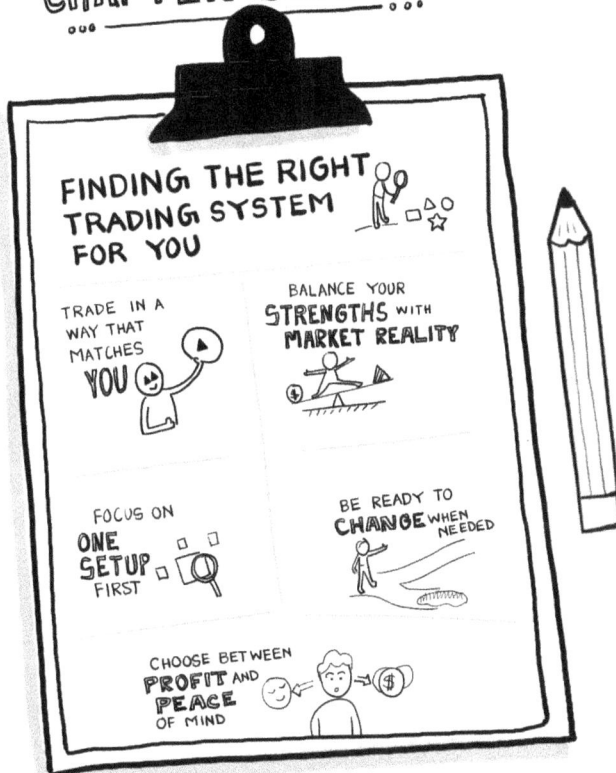

FINDING THE RIGHT TRADING SYSTEM FOR YOU

TRADE IN A WAY THAT MATCHES YOU

BALANCE YOUR STRENGTHS WITH MARKET REALITY

FOCUS ON ONE SETUP FIRST

BE READY TO CHANGE WHEN NEEDED

CHOOSE BETWEEN PROFIT AND PEACE OF MIND

PERSONALITY & BELIEFS

TRADING STRATEGY

MARKET REALITY

6

THE DIVERGENT TRADER

"The real voyage of discovery consists not in seeking new
landscapes, but in having new eyes."
– Marcel Proust

Being different is not easy. We are expected to behave a certain way since childhood. Schools teach us skills that help the "average" student succeed so we can fit into society. But the kids who see the world differently — the ones who challenge the rules and think outside the box — often get moulded to conform.

Over time, this conditioning stifles creativity. We start agreeing with popular beliefs and following the crowd. The result? Most people end up with similar outcomes in life. There is nothing necessarily wrong with that, but it limits our potential. It keeps us from seeing the world in new ways and making real breakthroughs. The same applies to trading. From the moment we start learning, we are taught certain rules and limitations. Everyone reads the same books, joins the same discussions, and develops similar strategies. Naturally, the results are also similar — average.

The choice is yours—stay in comfort or seek the truth?

But that does not have to be the case. Even though we have been trained to think within certain boundaries, we can rewire our brains to see the market differently. The right mindset can take your trading to the next level, helping you develop a deeper connection with the market and achieve exceptional results.

You will notice something interesting about top traders: they trade in ways that are unique to them. Their strategies do not always make sense to others, but they work because they are built on creativity and deep understanding. If you ask them about their success, they will often mention "discipline." Yes, discipline is important. But on its own, it will not make you great. You can be extremely disciplined and still get mediocre results. Meanwhile, a trader with a creative approach will find ways to leverage their knowledge and turn it into something extraordinary. Discipline is a low-risk, low-reward game. Creativity, on the other hand, is high-risk, high-reward. So, how do you tap into creativity when most of us have lost that spark we had as kids? It is easier than you think. With a few simple shifts in mindset, you can start unlocking doors you did not even realise were closed.

Here are a few things to incorporate into your trading that could help you immensely.

1. Immerse yourself in a creative environment

Surround yourself with what ignites your imagination, and creativity will follow.

One of the best ways to improve at something is to fully immerse yourself in it. The right environment can inspire creativity and push you to take action. A good starting point is your physical space. Imagine a workspace that makes you feel creative the moment you step into it. Simple changes — like vibrant colours, inspiring artwork, comfortable seating, or even a small plant — can spark new ideas and make your work feel more exciting. But your surroundings are not just about what is around you; they are also about *who* is around you. The people you spend time with shape your thinking more than you might realise. If you want to be more creative, surround yourself with creative people. There is a saying: *"You are the average of the five people you spend the most time with."* And it is true—when you are around people who think differently and push boundaries, it influences you to do the same. Look for those who see problems from unique angles, who challenge conventional thinking. Talk to them, learn from them, and let their approach to life open your mind to new possibilities.

Another way to boost creativity is to explore activities outside your main focus. Try painting, playing music, writing, or even cooking—anything that forces your brain to think differently. Creativity often comes from unexpected connections, and these activities can help you see things in a new light.

Most importantly, give yourself the freedom to experiment and make mistakes. Creativity flourishes in an environment where failure is not feared but embraced as part of the process. By shaping your surroundings, choosing the right influences, and allowing yourself to explore freely, you set the stage for creativity to thrive.

2. Question authority

Blind obedience is easy. True leadership begins with asking why.

One of the most important qualities you need as a trader to unlock creativity and innovation is *self-leadership*. It begins with accepting that no one has all the answers. We all figure things out as we go. Trading is not a fixed science where the same actions always lead to the same results. Every situation in the market is unique.

History might repeat itself, but never in the exact same way — it only rhymes. This means there are countless ways to make money in the market. Just because most traders follow one approach does not mean you have to. If you spot an opportunity that others overlook, do not hesitate to take it. Extraordinary results do not come from following the crowd; they come from independent thinking, questioning the norm, and having the confidence to lead yourself.

Self-leadership also means questioning authority — not for the sake of being rebellious, but to develop a mindset of healthy skepticism. Ask yourself, *"Is this really the best way?"* or *"Is there an alternative that makes more sense?"* The habit of questioning opens the door to new ideas and unique strategies. But none of this works unless you take full responsibility for your trading. You cannot blame the market, other traders, or external factors for your results. If you do, you will just be making excuses instead of improving. Once you accept that *your* decisions shape your success, you will start taking yourself more seriously. You will realise that you have the power to change the trajectory of your trading career.

When you develop self-leadership, you stop being just a follower of strategies — you become a leader in your own right. You gain the confidence to think differently, adapt, and create a trading style that truly works for *you*.

3. Have varied interests and exposure to other fields

It is hard to be different in contemporary times. Since childhood, we are expected to behave a certain way, to develop skills that help the "average" student succeed, and to fit into a system designed for the masses. But kids who think differently—the ones who see the world through their own lens and challenge the rules to create something extraordinary—often get moulded to conform. Over time, this conditioning makes us forget how to be creative. We start accepting what the majority believes and follow the crowd. As a result, most people end up with similar lives, similar choices, and similar outcomes. There is nothing inherently wrong with that, but it limits us. It caps our potential, keeping us from seeing the world as it truly is and achieving real breakthroughs—both as individuals and as a society.

The same pattern exists in trading. From the moment we step into this world, we are handed a set of "rules" about what works and what does not. Everyone studies the same materials, follows the same market narratives, and builds similar strategies. Naturally, most traders end up with average results. But it does not have to be that way. Even if you have been conditioned to believe certain limitations, you can rewire your brain to break out of those patterns. The traders who reach the highest levels are not just disciplined— they think differently. They develop unique market edges, use creativity to their advantage, and see opportunities others do not. Their ideas might not always make sense to the masses, but if you ask them what makes their system work, they will often say, *"discipline."* Yes, discipline is important, but on its own, it will not lead to greatness. You can be the most disciplined trader in the world and still not achieve extraordinary results. Meanwhile, a trader with a creative approach — one who builds leverage into their process — can reach a level far beyond someone relying on discipline alone. Think of it this way: *discipline is low-risk, low-reward. Creativity is high-risk, high-reward.*

So, how do you regain the creativity that most of us have lost over the years? It is easier than you think. With a few simple shifts, you can reopen doors that have been closed for too long. Here are a few ways to bring creativity into your trading and take things to the next level.

1. Do the "what if" exercise

"What if" is one of the most powerful phrases in my trading dictionary. It carries weight — both as a tool for progress and a source of self-doubt.

Used the wrong way, "what if" can be destructive. If it seeps into your execution, it leads to hesitation, second-guessing, and impulsive tweaks to your plan — usually driven by emotions rather than logic. But if you integrate it into your process, it can elevate your trading to the next level. Instead of letting "what if" create fear, use it to fuel curiosity:

- What if I tweak this entry slightly?
- What if I test this strategy in a different market condition?
- How can I extract more from this particular edge?

The more questions you ask, the more opportunities you create. Not every experiment will work, but each one gives you valuable insights. To get to these questions, you need to go deep. Study market history, analyse price behaviour, and pay close attention to the instruments you trade. Learn from live markets, try new things without expecting instant success, and accept that losses are part of the process.

The key? Do not be afraid of being wrong. You might be wrong 99 times, but that one breakthrough — the moment you uncover a high-potential strategy — can change everything. The problem is, most traders never get there because they fear failure too much. That brings us to a crucial mindset shift: You are not the outcomes of your trades. Becoming a consistently profitable trader is an ongoing cycle of trial, error, and refinement. It is about balancing discipline with adaptability — sticking to a structured approach while staying open to innovation. If you embrace "what if" in a controlled, methodical way, it becomes a tool for discovery, helping you push past limitations and unlock new levels of success.

2. You are not your outcomes

You are not the shadow of your failures.
You are the light that learns from them.

One of the biggest obstacles traders face is not the market — it is their own aversion to being wrong. We crave being right because we have tied our self-worth to our accuracy. A losing trade does not just feel like a financial setback; it feels like a personal failure. But if you let that mindset control you, you will only ever achieve average results. Let us be honest — you are not here to be just another trader in the crowd. The fear of being wrong is natural. It is a survival instinct. But the good news? You can rewire your brain to think differently.

To be a truly divergent trader, you must separate your self-worth from your outcomes.

Being wrong is not a sign of failure—it is a step in the learning process. Every mistake carries a lesson. And when you embrace that, you free yourself to take calculated risks, experiment, and refine your strategies without fear holding you back. The best traders do not just tolerate mistakes—they study them. They analyse what went wrong, extract insights, and adjust. This ability to detach from outcomes and focus on the process is what sets them apart. It is how they uncover unique market edges that most traders overlook.

A single trade—or even a series of trades—does not define you. What defines you is your resilience, your ability to adapt, and your commitment to improve. Being a divergent trader means daring to be different, thinking beyond conventional wisdom, and having the courage to challenge the status quo. It means letting go of the need to always be right and embracing the journey of continuous growth. In the long run, it is not about being right all the time. It is about evolving into a trader who sees, thinks, and operates differently—and that is where real success lies.

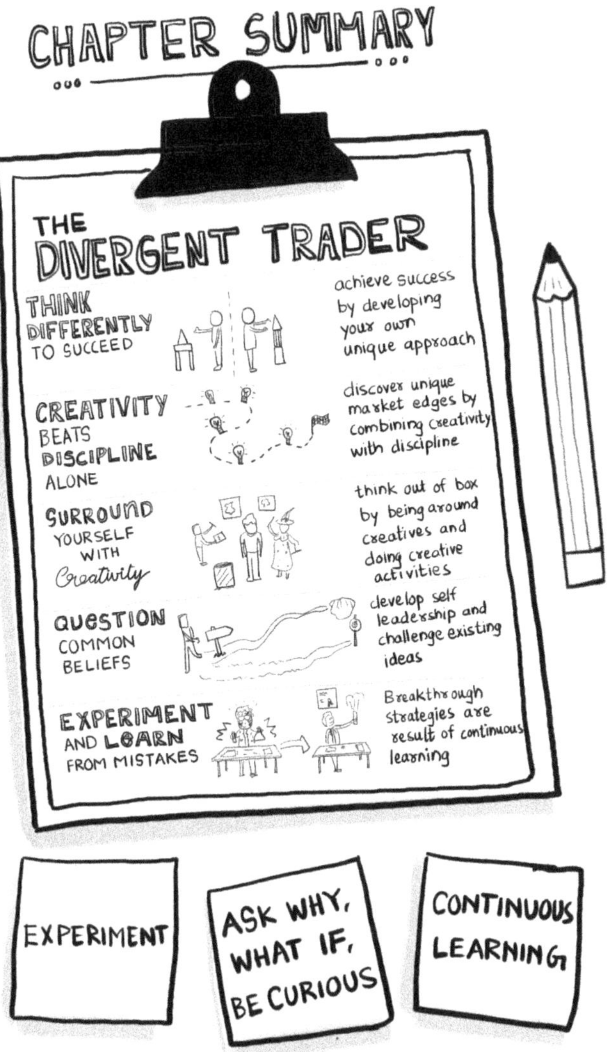
CHAPTER SUMMARY
THE DIVERGENT TRADER
THINK DIFFERENTLY TO SUCCEED
achieve success by developing your own unique approach
CREATIVITY BEATS DISCIPLINE ALONE
discover unique market edges by combining creativity with discipline
SURROUND YOURSELF WITH Creativity
think out of box by being around creatives and doing creative activities
QUESTION COMMON BELIEFS
develop self leadership and challenge existing ideas
EXPERIMENT AND LEARN FROM MISTAKES
Breakthrough strategies are result of continuous learning
EXPERIMENT
ASK WHY, WHAT IF, BE CURIOUS
CONTINUOUS LEARNING

7

How to Make Big Leaps in Trading

"Success isn't just about what you achieve; it's about what
you consistently do. Small intentional steps taken daily
lead to the greatest results."
— John C. Maxwell

There are many ways to live life, but they generally fall into two approaches: going with the flow—letting circumstances dictate your achievements, emotions, and direction—or living intentionally, taking control of your actions and actively shaping your future. Trading is no different. Some treat it like a hobby, dabbling here and there, unaffected by whether they succeed or not. They drift with the market, hoping things will work out. But if you want to accelerate your growth as a trader, that mindset will not cut it. Success does not come from passivity—it comes from intentionality. Every action you take should have a purpose, a clear intent to refine and improve some aspect of your trading. Such traders succeed faster than the rest.

You will often hear, "It takes years to get good at trading." No, it does not. What you need is not time—it is deliberate practice. This is what focused effort designed to produce specific results looks like.

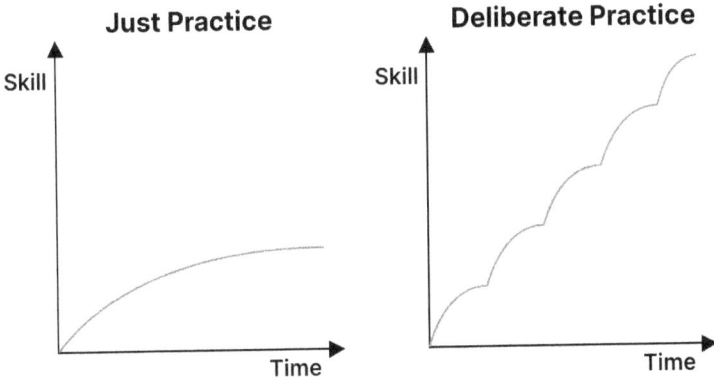

Just Practice

Skill

Time

Deliberate Practice

Skill

Time

In this chapter, we will break down the key strategies that will help you achieve that. Here is a preview of what is ahead:

1. Focus on doing one thing right at a time
2. Plan before you execute
3. Build a database
4. Focus on the process, not the P&L
5. Lower the downside

By adopting these strategies in your trading arsenal, you can transform your trading approach and achieve the success you have been striving for.

Let us explore each of these methods in detail, so you can start making intentional, impactful changes to your trading practice.

1. Focus on doing one thing right at a time

Half-done work, half-baked results. Pick one, go all in.

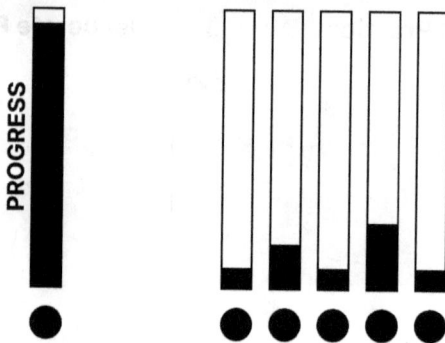

The biggest reason most traders struggle to make big leaps is distraction. They try to improve everything at once — entries, exits, risk management, stock selection — all at the same time. And that is the problem. When you focus on too many things, you end up improving nothing. That is why you need a singular focus. Instead of spreading yourself thin, identify one thing that, if improved, would have the biggest impact on your trading. Maybe it is refining your entries, reading market conditions better, or developing rock-solid discipline. Whatever it is, lock in on it and give it your full attention. Think of a laser — it is powerful because it focuses light into one concentrated beam. Your efforts should be the same. Pick one skill, master it, and then move on to the next. For example, if you are working on better entries, ignore everything else for a while. Study historical setups, backtest your strategies, and refine your entry criteria. Once you feel confident, shift focus to the next area of improvement. This step-by-step approach builds a strong foundation. Instead of trying to be perfect at everything all at once, you improve one thing at a time—and over time, these small wins stack up to massive progress.

So, if you are feeling stuck in your trading, ask yourself: *What is the one thing that, if improved, would make the biggest difference?* Focus on that. Master it. Then move on. That is how you make real breakthroughs.

2. Plan before you execute

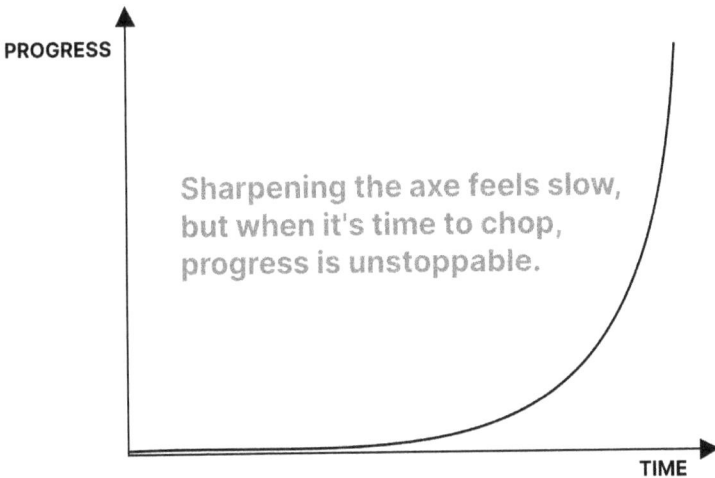

"Give me six hours to chop down a tree and I will spend the first four sharpening the axe."
—Abraham Lincoln

The most important aspect of achieving great results is planning! It might seem like something that is obvious, most people just want to jump into the arena without any plan because they are so pumped up, distracted by the potential outcomes they can achieve if they do come out to be the winner. What they do not know is that without a plan, they are setting themselves up for failure. You need a concrete idea of what you want to achieve in your trading and how you are going to achieve it. It should not be just vague things, but concrete and precise steps you have to take in order to achieve those particular results.

First, let us talk about what a plan should include. It should have clearly defined goals. What are you aiming for? Is it a specific return on investment, or a certain amount of profit? Or maybe it is about building consistency in your trading performance. Whatever your goals are, write them down. Make sure they are specific, measurable, achievable, relevant, and time-bound (SMART). The next step is to develop a strategy to achieve those specific goals which involves deciding what kind of trader you want to be. Are you a day trader, swing trader, or long-term investor? You must make that distinction before you go ahead as each approach requires a different set of skills and tools. Once you have identified your trading style, you need to choose a trading system that fits that style. This particular system should include criteria for entering and exiting trades, risk management rules, and a method for analysing the market. Once you have a strategy, the next step is to backtest it, which means running your trading system through historical data to see how it would have performed. This step helps you identify any flaws in your system and refine it before you start trading with real money. Many people skip this step. Do not do that—it is like practising before the big game. With a refined strategy, now you are ready to create a detailed trading plan. This plan should outline your daily routine, how you will scan for trades, your criteria for entering and exiting trades, how you will manage risk, and how you will record and review your trades. It should also include contingency plans for when things go wrong, because in trading, things can and do go wrong.

Once you have this whole blueprint of how you are going to approach trading, things are going to work out in your favour better than you could have imagined, you must keep in mind that most people do not even complete one of these aforementioned steps, so you see how low the bar has been set, you just have to put in the work right when it is necessary and then it is just simply executing that plan in live markets.

3. Building a database is the easiest thing you can do to improve your trading results

I have emphasised the need to build a trading database, a playbook, before. I might sound like a broken record at this point, but if I could recommend one thing that could literally change the trajectory of your trading career, it would be to focus all your energy for the next few months on just building your playbook and nothing else. The problem with most traders is that they like the action, the thrill of being in a trade. They like the idea of potential profits they could extract from the market, but the thing is, most of them are delusional. They have no concrete edge, no plan for how they are going to attain success in the market. They do random stuff, so they get random results. Most people never seem to stop and ask themselves, "What am I doing?" Once you become self-aware about your current reality and know that the only path to success is by taking the right set of actions and putting in hard work, everything changes. You cannot escape doing the work.

Overview	Playbook Rules	Executed Trades	Missed Trades	Notes

Net P&L ⓘ
$108,993.08

Trades ⚙
124

Win Rate % ⓘ
75%

Profit Factor ⓘ
283.21

Missed Trades ⓘ
31

Rules Followed ⓘ
73%

Average Winner ⓘ
$36,459.76

Average Loser
-$386.21

Largest Profit
$74,882.24

Largest Loss
-$386.21

Daily Net Cumulative P&L

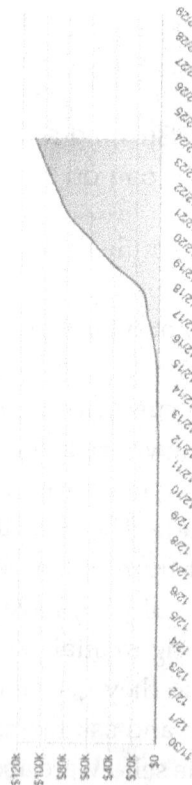

$120k
$100k
$80k
$60k
$40k
$20k
$0

7/30 1/31 12/1 12/2 12/3 12/4 12/6 12/7 12/8 12/9 12/10 12/11 12/12 12/13 12/14 12/15 12/16 12/17 12/18 12/19 12/20 12/21 12/22 12/23 12/24 12/25 12/26 12/27 12/28 12/29

Stats	Playbooks

Net P&L ⓘ
$1,649.94

Playbook
Create new playbook

Opening Drive 📄

Rules Followed
CHECK ALL

8 / 9

SETUP CONTEXT

☑ Purpose of this setup is to capitalize on the pump (drive) that occurs right at open due to an increase in PVOL, shorts getting squeezed off liquidity, etc. This is supposed to be a quick trade — like a "scalp".

BASIC CONTEXT

☑ RVOL on the underlying is at 1.4 or higher

LIQUIDITY CONTEXT

☑ Showing high long-term liquidity

☑ We see absorption right at open

☐ Bidding higher

VOLUME CONTEXT

☑ Large buy volume / Large sell volume with no follow through right at open

☑ VERY fast pace

Trading is no different than any other job, business, or sport in the sense that the top achievers in those domains are the ones who have given their all to honing their skills. They are not just doing it for the thrill or fun of it but because they have a mission: the mission to become the best. Only the top 0.001% enjoy 99% of the rewards. That is the hard truth you have to make peace with. Most people do not work that hard; they think they are smart enough or they have figured it out. But have they? Well, your account equity does not lie. If all you have is a bunch of opinions about how smart you are with nothing to show for it, then you are not that smart. So, sit down and focus on giving everything you can to become good at this game. The biggest jump you can take in that direction is by building a playbook. One aspect of building a playbook is to be as thorough with your "plays" or "setups" as you can. Most people would have their charts in their playbook look like this: a bunch of scattered notes and vague recollections. That is not good enough. While a lot of setups look great and obvious in your playbook, you must keep in mind that hindsight bias is also at play here. Hindsight bias is when you look at past events and believe they were predictable, even if they were not at the time. It is easy to look at historical charts and think you would have easily spotted the setup.

This bias can give you a false sense of confidence. To combat this, you need to be extremely detailed in your playbook. Document not only the chart pattern but also the market conditions, your state of mind, and any other relevant factors in great detail. This will help you understand why a setup worked or did not work and will make your playbook a powerful tool for future trades. Building a trading database is not glamorous. It is not exciting, and it is certainly not the quick path to making money. But it is the foundation on which successful trading careers are built. If you take time to meticulously document your setups and learn from each trade, you are setting yourself up for long-term success. So, get started on your playbook today. Your future self will thank you.

4. Focus on the process, not the profit and loss

Mastery is a byproduct of process, not obsession with results.

- ✅ Followed the Entry Plan
- ✅ Followed the Exit Plan
- ✅ Managed Risk
- ✅ Remained Composed
- ✅ Executed without hesitation

If you want to make big leaps in your trading the first thing you have to keep in mind as a trader is, you cannot force good results. Good results are actually an outcome of having a good process. If your process is not good, trying to force good outcomes is like trying to steer a car with a broken wheel. It just will not work well, no matter how hard you try.

I have experienced this first-hand as a trader. In my early years, I made the mistake of setting a goal to make a certain amount of money every month. But as James Clear says, "we do not rise to the level of our goals; we fall to the level of our systems." Unless you have solid systems and knowledge in place, trying to force results is just going to lead to mistakes. Learning takes time, and building systems takes time. It is a long journey that cannot be shortened by reading books or taking courses. You need real experience to take full advantage of the edges you have created for yourself.

We have two main tools to learn about the markets: history (what has happened in the past) and what is happening now. With each new market cycle, you learn new things about yourself and the markets. This knowledge is just as valuable as studying market history. That is why having a lot of screen time is so important if you want to achieve good results in the market. The more you watch and participate in the markets, the more you understand the nuances and patterns that cannot be learned from books alone. It is about developing a feel for the market, which only comes with time and experience. So, focus on refining your process and systems, and the results will follow naturally.

5. The trick is lowering the downside!

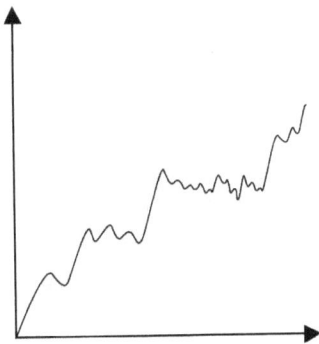

Smaller dips → Better risk management Deeper corrections → Harder to recover

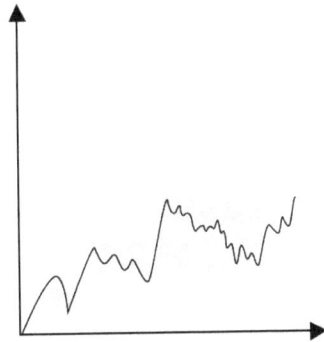

Initially, I struggled a lot in trading, just like everyone does. I went through every resource, every book, podcast, and course—anything I could get my hands on. But nothing helped me improve my results beyond a certain point. I was

improving, but it was a lot slower than I would have liked. Then suddenly, my trading took a big turn for the better! The insight came after I studied the data from my trading journal. I figured out that if I could stop my trading losses from going above a certain point, I would make about 5 times the returns I had been making. Just cutting the top 20% of my losses would have led to massive improvements in my system, even after accounting for the potential profits I might have missed by cutting some of the losers. This was a huge revelation for me at the time. I believed that to enhance my trading results, I had to catch bigger moves and find multibagger stocks. But that was not true. I could have achieved respectable results even if I had simply lowered my drawdowns, that is, reduced my downside. Limiting the downside automatically helps produce better returns. That is why it is said that you can have the best setups and the best stock-picking skills in town, but if your risk management is poor, you are only going to get subpar results. Your job as a trader should not just be to focus on improving the upside but also on lowering your downside. Do not just remain a stock picker; become a risk manager first and see the change in your trading.

Once I started focusing on minimising my losses, everything changed. I no longer felt the pressure to hit home runs with every trade. Instead, I concentrated on protecting my capital and making consistent, smaller gains. This shift in mindset made trading much less stressful and more sustainable over the long term. The key was realising that managing the downside was more important than chasing big wins. By limiting my losses, I automatically improved my overall returns. It was a simple but powerful insight: avoiding big losses helped me stay in the game longer and gave me more opportunities to profit.

One practical way to lower the downside is by setting strict stops on your open positions. This means deciding in advance the maximum amount you are willing to lose on a trade and sticking to it. You must stay disciplined and not let emotions take over when a trade goes against you.

Another method is to avoid overtrading and only taking fewer, higher-quality trades which can reduce the chances of incurring large and frequent losses. It is better to be selective and patient, waiting for the best opportunities rather than trying to be in the market all the time.

The bottom line is that by focusing on limiting your downside, you create a more stable and profitable trading journey. It is not about making huge gains quickly; it is about preserving your capital and steadily growing it over time. Becoming a risk manager first and a stock picker second can transform your trading results.

CHAPTER SUMMARY

HOW TO MAKE BIG LEAPS IN TRADING

FOCUS ON ONE THING AT A TIME — DON'T TRY TO IMPROVE EVERYTHING ONCE

PLAN BEFORE YOU EXECUTE — SET CLEAR GOALS / DEVELOP A STRATEGY / BACK TEST IT / HAVE A DAILY ROUTINE

BUILD A DATABASE (PLAYBOOK) — RECORD YOUR TRADES, SET UPS AND MARKET CONDITIONS

FOCUS ON PROCESS NOT PROFIT — BUILD SOLID SYSTEMS / STICK TO THEM / RESULTS COME NATURALLY

LOWER THE DOWNSIDE — MANAGE LOSSES / PROTECT CAPITAL / MINIMIZE BIG DRAW DOWNS

PROCESS

FOCUS

MANAGE LOSS

8

Using Behavioural Finance to Develop an Antifragile Trading Approach

In my first few years of trading, I felt like I was struggling just like everyone else. It was not that I was not trying hard enough—I was. I tried everything! I followed new trading mentors, read a bunch of books, signed up for different courses, and spent countless hours studying charts, hoping to find that one missing piece of the puzzle that would make everything fall into place. But the more I learned, the more confused I became. Nothing seemed to work. In fact, I became so overwhelmed that I almost froze (not literally, but you get what I mean). I was scared to take trades because I started thinking, "What if this is the end of my trading journey?" It was a frustrating time. I kept questioning everything—my decisions, strategy, and even my ability to succeed in the market.

But then something changed. And when I say, "something clicked," I do not mean it happened overnight. Even when I was struggling, one habit never changed. I would fill out my trading journal every single day, without fail. And that habit, was the key. By keeping track of my own actions and what was happening in the market, I started to see patterns. I became more aware of not just what I was doing, but also what other traders were doing.

One day, while reviewing my journal, something hit me. Most traders either lose money or just break even. And the ones who consistently make money? They are rare. I asked myself: "What if I stop doing what most traders do? What if I try to understand how normal, rational people behave in the market, and then do the exact opposite?" That realisation changed everything for me. It was like I suddenly saw a door that had been invisible before. From that moment on, I started building a trading system based on doing what most traders cannot or will not do. And the best part? The system put me in a position of strength almost automatically. This was not about finding a magical strategy. It was based on something much deeper — human psychology. I realised that the market often moves in ways that reflect how regular people think and react under pressure. So, I started studying those behaviours, using ideas from behavioural finance to see how people act when the market is stressful. Then, I adjusted my approach to take advantage of those patterns.

Here are a few key principles I discovered as I dug deeper. These lessons came from observing what the majority of traders do — and then figuring out how to turn those behaviours into opportunities for myself.

1. They think only systems that have a higher win rate can make money

One of the biggest misunderstandings among retail traders is the idea that to make money in the market, you need a system that wins most of the time. Many traders believe that the only way to be profitable is by having a high win rate. But in my opinion, that could not be further from the truth. In fact, this belief is one of the main reasons why so many retail traders end up losing money. What most people do not realise is that they do not actually understand what makes a trading system profitable. They get too focused on win rate, thinking that it is the most important factor. But win rate is just one part of the bigger picture. There are other, far more important factors that decide whether a system will make money over time. If you break it down, profitability comes from a simple equation:

Edge = win rate * average winner – loss rate * average loser

Look at that formula.

It has four key parts: win rate, loss rate, average winner, and average loser.

But most traders focus only on one – win rate – and ignore the rest. They assume that if they can increase their win rate, they will automatically become profitable. But in reality, it is not that simple. When traders go searching for a high win rate system, they quickly realise it is much more difficult than they expected.

High Win-rate %

Choose 2

Big Winners   Low Risk

The market is highly efficient, which means there are not many obvious advantages just waiting to be found. And even if there were, big players with deep pockets and advanced technology have probably already discovered and used them. So, chasing a high win rate system is like chasing a mirage — it looks promising, but once you get there, it is not what you thought it would be. Even if, by some stroke of luck, you manage to backtest a strategy that shows a high win rate, there is no guarantee it will work in live trading.

It is easy to adjust a strategy to fit past data and make it look good, but the real test is how it performs in real-time. Markets change, conditions shift, and a strategy that worked in the past might completely fail when real money is on the line. This is why experienced traders do not focus too much on win rate. Instead, they prefer systems that may have a lower win rate but produce much bigger profits on their winning trades compared to their losing ones. These systems are stronger — they can handle some losses and still come out ahead. They do not need to win all the time because when they do win, the gains are large enough to cover the losses. In other words, these systems are built to survive the ups and downs of the market. Even if the strategy's edge is not as strong as it looked in the backtest, it can still manage risk and give more stable results over time.

On the other hand, a high win rate system is much more fragile. If just a few trades do not go as planned, the whole strategy can fall apart, leading to bigger losses than expected. So, if you want to avoid this kind of frustration in your trading, stop chasing high win rate systems. Instead, focus on strategies that are built to create big winners. It is not about how many times you win — it is about how much you make when you do.

2. They think there is some secret to making profits

Another big misunderstanding that many traders have is the belief that there is some secret formula for making money in the market. They think that to succeed, you need a special ability to predict exactly where prices will go. It is almost as if they believe only a few "chosen ones" have access to hidden knowledge that the rest of us do not.

But that is not how it works! I speak from experience. I am a consistently profitable trader, and I have met plenty of others who are making serious money in this business. Not a single one of us believes we have some special insight that others do not. You would think people with incredibly high IQs—people who probably know way more about economics, markets, and data than any of us traders do would be the ones making the most money, right? But strangely, that is often not the case. What I have learned is that being super smart is not a requirement for success in trading. Of course, intelligence helps, but it is not the most important thing. It is similar to how there is no "secret" to getting healthy, staying fit, or doing well on an exam. You already know what you need to do—eat well, exercise regularly, and study hard. The formula is right in front of you. The same goes for trading.

The problem is that most traders are simply lazy, and they do not understand the importance of discipline. These two things—laziness and lack of discipline—are the main reasons why most people fail in the market. First, they do not put in the time and effort needed to build a profitable trading system. Creating a system is not exciting work. It involves hours of studying charts, writing down observations, keeping track of setups, and testing different strategies.

Most traders skip this part. They think they can just figure it out as they go or that some shortcut will magically appear. Even the few who actually do build a system, face another big problem: discipline. When it is time to trade live, they cannot stick to the plan. The urge to break the rules, chase losses, or trade based on emotions is just too strong. Once you understand that most trading failures come down to these two mistakes — not putting in the work and not staying disciplined — you start to see the way forward. This is the foundation you need to focus on if you want to become a consistently profitable trader (CPT). Realising this is what will set you apart from the crowd.

3. They self-sabotage

What you tell yourself matters.
If you believe you'll fail,
you'll make sure you do.

One thing I have noticed about the top 0.1% of traders is that they are completely comfortable with who they are and how they trade. They have made peace with the ups and downs of the market. When they win, they do not get overconfident or let it boost their ego. And when they lose, they do not get frustrated or upset. Their self-worth is not tied to their trading results. A bad trading day does not ruin the rest of their life, and they do not take it out on the people around them.

If you look at most traders, it is a completely different story. They are constantly fighting with themselves. They are so frustrated with their results that every time they lose money, they end up making things worse. They think, "I must be an idiot," or "Maybe I deserve to lose," or "I'll never make it in trading." What they do not realise is that words have power. And no, this is not some mystical idea—it is just how the mind works.

When you keep telling yourself something over and over, you start to believe it. It becomes part of your thinking, and before you know it, your actions start matching those beliefs. If you always tell yourself that you are a failure or that you do not deserve success, you will act in ways that make those things true. I am not saying that just thinking positive thoughts will suddenly make you a confident trader. But it will help you create the right mindset for change. Your mind will not fight against you when you try to improve, and setbacks will not feel like the end of the world.

So how do you start changing? Begin with two simple things:

1. Try to see things in a positive way.
2. Be as kind to yourself as you would be to a friend.

If you make a mistake or lose money, take a step back and ask yourself: Would you say something cruel to a friend who made the same mistake? Would you call them an idiot? Probably not. So why do that to yourself? You will not change this overnight. There will still be moments when you feel like you do not deserve success, or that you are not good enough. Even you do not fully know how great you can be. You just have not tapped into that potential yet. The way you start unlocking it is by showing up every day, putting in the work, and learning from your mistakes. Success in trading is not about being perfect—it is about making progress. And that progress starts with treating yourself with the respect you deserve.

4. They rely on hunches

A well-defined process removes any room for potential errors.

What to do if one of my holdings gap down below my stop loss:

- Wait for the first 5 mins to let the volatility settle.

- Put stop below 5 min low.

- Exit if the TSL gets hit.

- If the TSL does not get hit by the end of the day keep Low of that day as your stop

Clear steps to navigate if this scenario plays out.

(Hypothetical example)

After more than a decade in trading, I have seen all kinds of traders. Some make decisions based on experience, while others follow strict rules. There are scalpers, day traders, swing traders, and long-term investors. But most consistently profitable traders do not rely on gut feelings or guesses. They follow a system with clear, well-defined rules. Sure, some traders have been in the game for decades and can trust their instincts. But even they follow certain rules. Their intuition comes from years of experience. If you are not at that level yet and you do not have a solid set of rules, trading will feel like an uphill battle.

If you are making trades just because you "have a feeling" about the market, you are probably not going to last long. No matter your trading style—whether it is day trading, swing trading, or long-term investing — you need clear rules for everything you do. These rules give you structure and focus, helping you find the best opportunities in the market. To stay on track, you need a solid trading plan. Think of it like a roadmap for your trading decisions. Here is a quick overview of what that plan should include:

1. **Define your trading system:** Are you going to be a trend follower, someone who jumps in with the momentum? Or maybe a counter-trend trader who thrives on reversals? You need to know what type of system you are going to follow because it forms the foundation of your trading strategy.

2. **Choose your tools:** You have to decide which tools you will use on your charts to identify setups. Will you rely on moving averages, volume indicators, trend lines, or volume weighted average price (VWAP)? Pick your weapons carefully because these tools are going to help you make sense of the market.

3. **Timeframes and instruments:** Which timeframe will you be trading on? Are you looking at the 5-minute chart, or do you prefer a daily or weekly view? And which instruments will you trade — stocks, options, futures, or something else entirely? Be clear about these details.

4. **Entry and exit rules:** You also need well-defined rules for entering and exiting trades. When do you pull the trigger on a setup? What criteria must be met before you take the trade? And once you are in, how will you manage the position — when do you exit, whether for a profit or a loss?

This is just a brief outline, but your trading plan should cover all these points in detail. The goal is to make everything clear so that when a situation comes up in the market, you already know what to do. No hesitation, no second-guessing as you have already decided in advance. Having clear rules will help you in two big ways. First, it will boost your confidence. Once your rules are set, you can backtest your strategy—run it through past market data to see how it would have performed. Since your strategy follows consistent rules, backtesting will give you a much better idea of how it might perform in real trading.

Second, having rules will help you stay disciplined. It takes emotions out of the picture because your trades are no longer based on gut feelings but on a solid plan. You will not get caught up in fear or greed because your decisions have already been made. In the end, trading is not about predicting the future or finding some magic formula. It is about having a system, following it, and executing your trades with precision. That is how you move from guessing to trading like a professional.

5. They are scared

Fear doesn't vanish with more knowledge. It fades with action.

Most retail traders operate from a place of fear. They fear losing money, making mistakes, and deep down, they fear that they might never actually succeed. And this fear shows up in their trading—taking small, cautious positions, even when they know enough to justify trading bigger. They know they could do better. They see the potential to break free from playing small and rise to the top 0.1%. Yet, something holds them back, keeping them stuck in a cycle of hesitation.

Most never stop to ask: Why? Why do they keep limiting themselves? Why can they not break free? The answer is simple: they do not trust their system because they have not put in the work to build that trust. Many traders dream of reaching the top, but they are not willing to do what it takes to get there.

They want the rewards without the effort, the success without the grind. Nothing external is stopping them from trading bigger. No mysterious force is holding them back. They are the ones standing in their own way. Once you truly understand this, the path forward becomes clear. You stop making excuses, start building real confidence—the kind that comes from putting in the work. That is what allows you to grow your size, stomach bigger drawdowns, and take larger profits without flinching. Because in the end, trading is not just about skill—it is about having the courage to step up when it matters most.

6. They lose a lot – a few times

One of the biggest reasons traders fail is not that they do not know how to trade—it is that they take massive losses compared to their wins. They might have a good grasp of the market, but there is an invisible line where the ego takes over. That is where everything starts to unravel. When you let your ego dictate your trades, you set yourself up for disaster. The moment you care more about being right than being profitable, you are headed down a slippery slope. You start holding on to losing trades longer than you should.

The setup might have looked great at first, but when the trade no longer makes sense, you need to cut it. Yet most traders cannot. They hold on, convincing themselves the market will turn around because of their ego. They cannot accept the loss and refuse to admit they were wrong, even though being wrong is just part of the game. What they do not realise is that trading is not about being right all the time—it is a probability game. You can follow every rule, execute perfectly, and still take a loss. That is just how it works.

But many traders do not think that way. They come in with the mindset that effort guarantees results—like in a normal job. In most professions, if you work hard, you see progress. Trading does not work like that. You can do everything right and still lose money. And that is where traders start to panic. They widen their stops, hoping the trade will turn. They hold losers longer than they should, telling themselves that they will break even in just a little more time. When the losses get too big, they stop being traders altogether and turn into long-term investors—bag-holding losing positions for months or years, waiting for the market to "come back." This is the trap. Most of the time, these traders do fine—taking small wins here and there. But all it takes is a few catastrophic losses to wipe them out completely. Do not make that mistake.

Trading is not about avoiding losses; it is about managing them. Losses are inevitable—the key is making sure they are never so big that they take you out of the game. The problem is not losing. It is how you handle losing. Most traders cannot take a loss. They will do anything to avoid it—widen stops, refuse to use stops at all, take tiny position sizes to "play it safe," or hold on to losers way too long. And all of those behaviours lead straight to blowups.

The only way to separate yourself from the pack is to do the opposite. Do not let your ego get in the way. If the trade is not working, cut it. If the thesis is no longer valid, get out. Do not hold on to losers just because you are afraid to take the hit. Focus on the process. Follow your rules. Respect the probability game that trading is. Do that, and your losses will be manageable. You will not take the kind of hits that wipe you out. And that is the key to longevity in this business. Most traders fail because they think winning means outsmarting the market. It does not. Winning comes down to discipline, risk management, and following the process. The sooner you accept that, the sooner you will start seeing real progress.

So do not be the trader who loses a lot just a few times. Be the trader who controls their losses, stays in the game, and makes it to the other side. That is how you win.

7. They keep repeating their mistakes

# Trade no.	Trade Result	Remarks
1	Loss	Late Entry
2	Loss	Same mistake
3	Loss	Same mistake
4	Loss	Same mistake
5	Loss	Same mistake
6	Loss	Same mistake
7	Loss	Same mistake
8	Loss	Same mistake
9	Loss	Same mistake
10	Loss	Same mistake

One of the biggest reasons traders never break into profitability is their tendency to repeat the same mistakes—

over and over. They mess up, feel bad for a few days, then shrug it off... only to do the exact same thing next time. It is a cycle that never ends. They might say, "Damn, I messed up again," but that guilt? It is just a coping mechanism. It lets them vent for a moment, but once the feeling fades, the lesson is lost. That is the real problem. Trading is not about feeling bad when you make mistakes — it is about learning from them. The first step is not self-pity; it is figuring out why it happened. Was it unavoidable? Or was it a mistake you could have prevented? If it is the latter, that is where your focus needs to be — not on guilt, but on fixing the root cause.

A lot of traders believe success is about sharpening their strengths, perfecting their A-game. But that is only half the battle. The real work? It is in plugging the leaks — the smaller mistakes that quietly drag you down and keep you from reaching your full potential.

I have seen traders in the market for years making the same rookie mistakes as on day one. Think about that. Do they really believe some magic moment is coming that will suddenly make them profitable? The truth is, trading is one of the hardest games out there. If you do not constantly improve, trust me — someone else is doing it. And they will be the ones taking your money. This is not a game for the mentally lazy. No, you do not need to be a genius, or know some secret, ultra-profitable system. What you do need is to stop being reckless, stop repeating the same mistakes, and start fixing what is holding you back. That is your job.

Do not sit around feeling sorry for yourself, wondering why you are not making it. Ask yourself, "Have I actually done everything I can to improve? Have I given it my all?" If the answer is no, then good news — it is not too late. Get back to work and fix what needs fixing. That is the only way you will become a winner in this game.

8. They have a negative outlook of the world

One of the most common things among traders who never make it is a negative outlook. They believe the game is rigged, the odds are stacked against them, and that everything—from the markets to the people around them—is out to get them. These traders feel trapped. They see others succeed, but instead of feeling inspired, they feel bitter and resentful. Deep down, they have convinced themselves that no matter what they do, the result will always be the same: failure. And that frustration turns into a kind of quiet, simmering anger—at the market, successful traders, and the world itself.

But here is the thing: nobody starts with this negative mindset. Most traders begin full of hope, energy, and excitement. So, what changes?

Two things: the environment they are in and the content they consume. The conversations they engage in, the information from the media they consume, and the people they surround themselves with. Spend enough time around traders who complain, blame, and make excuses, and it will rub off on you. Negativity is contagious. Slowly, you start seeing the world through their lens. You start telling yourself that nothing is your fault, that you are a victim in all of this. The harsh truth is that such a mindset is just a defence mechanism. When the pressure gets too much, the brain looks for someone or something to blame. And blaming the world is way easier than admitting you need to change. The moment you start blaming the market, you lose focus. You stop pushing yourself. You convince yourself that the problem is not you—it is everything else. That is when you start saying things like:

"The market is rigged."
"Retail traders cannot win."
"Technical analysis does not work."

But these are just excuses — signs of a mind that has stopped searching for solutions and settled into resentment. And the moment you do that, you lose the one thing you need to succeed: creative energy. Because winning in trading is not about blaming the world. It is about taking ownership. About looking in the mirror and saying, "I control my results. Nobody else." The market does not care about your excuses. It only cares about whether you are willing to do what it takes to succeed.

CHAPTER SUMMARY

USING BEHAVIOURAL SCIENCE TO BUILD ANTIFRAGILE SYSTEM

FEAR KEEPS TRADERS SMALL

THEY HESITATE TO TRADE BIGGER DESPITE HAVING THE SKILLS

BIG LOSSES KILL PROGRESS

HOLDING ONTO BAD TRADES WIPES OUT MONTHS OF GAINS

REPEATING MISTAKES

FEELING BAD ISN'T ENOUGH, FIXING WEAKNESS IS THE KEY

MINDSET MATTERS

BLAMING THE MARKETS KEEPS TRADERS STUCK, TAKE RESPONSIBILITY

DISCIPLINE DRIVES SUCCEESS

WINNING TRADERS FOCUS ON RISK MANAGEMENT AND CONSISTENCY

FEAR

MINDSET

DISCIPLINE

SECTION III

IMPROVING YOUR SYSTEM

"Success is the sum of small efforts, repeated day in and day out."
— Robert Collier

Once you have a trading process in place, the next step is continuous improvement. This section is dedicated to refining your system, enhancing your discipline, and developing the adaptability needed to thrive in an ever-changing market.

In this section we will discuss how to stay focused amidst distractions and the importance of sticking to your plan, even when faced with uncertainty. The key here is going to be to fine-tune your approach, making incremental improvements that lead to consistent success over time.

9

TRADING DISCIPLINE: YOUR UNSEEN EDGE

"We must all suffer one of two things: the pain of discipline or the pain of regret."
— Jim Rohn

I have a friend who was an absolute monster in the markets. For nearly a decade, he crushed it—year after year, triple-digit returns were just normal for him. He made it look effortless. His trading buddies called him 'The Golden Trader'. His strategy was simple, yet deadly effective. He was a momentum trader, always locked in on the fastest-moving names. His charting skills were next level, his instincts razor-sharp. He could spot trends before most even saw them forming, and when the moment came, he pulled the trigger—no hesitation.

Until it all fell apart.

He did not just take a hit—he got wrecked. A single series of mistakes cost him nearly half of his account. It was a blow so brutal that he stepped away from trading entirely. And it all started with something small. One day, he broke his own rule. He took a position bigger than usual—justified it as a "high-confidence trade." But confidence was not the issue. Overconfidence was. The trade went against him. No big deal—he had seen this before. Only this time, he did not cut it off in time. He held on to it, telling himself that the market would turn. That he just needed to "give it some room." That was the beginning of the end. The loss spiralled. He started revenge trading. Chasing setups that were not really there. Taking trades without analysis, purely on emotion— overleveraged, undisciplined, completely out of control. His once-steady equity curve—the one that climbed for years without fail—started cracking. And then, it collapsed.

The thing is, having a hard edge—a great strategy, sharp technical skills—that is essential. But it is not enough. If your soft edge is not solid—your mindset, discipline, ability to stick to your rules—then eventually, the market will expose you. That is exactly what happened to him. In the end, it was not the market that beat him. He beat himself.

In this chapter we will discuss the importance of discipline, how traders ignore it and pay the price, and how you can cultivate discipline in your trading.

BULL MARKET: A BOON OR BANE?

It is often said that *when* you start trading can play a big role in determining whether you go on to become a successful trader or just another statistic. And I fully agree. I have noticed that traders who start in tough market conditions tend to do better in the long run than those who have an easy ride in the beginning.

Take a swing trader, for example. In a bull market, opportunities seem endless. Even a beginner can make good money in a short span because bull markets are forgiving.

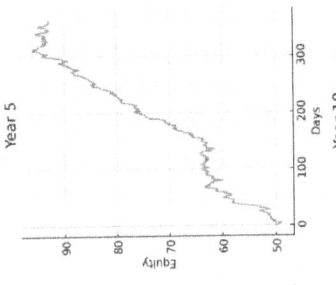

Year 5

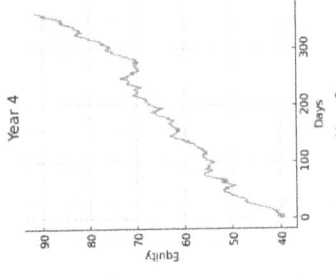

Year 4

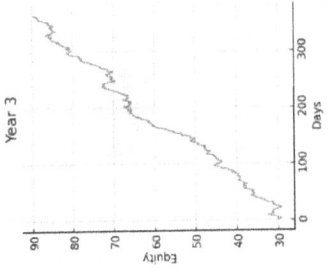

Year 3

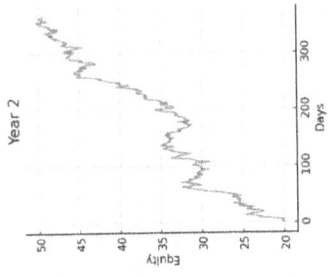

Year 2

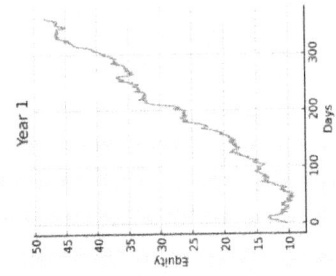

Year 1

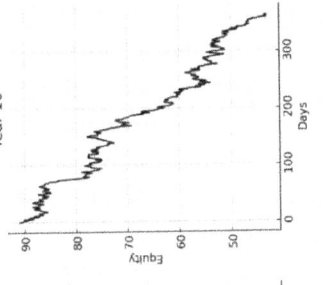

Year 10

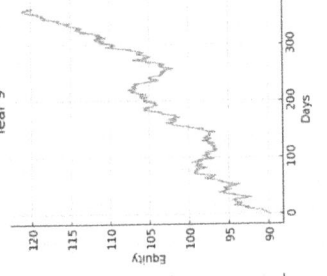

Year 9

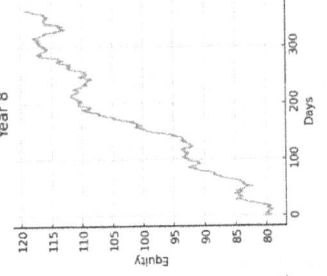

Year 8

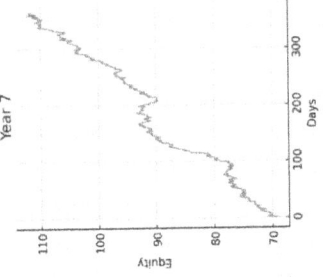

Year 7

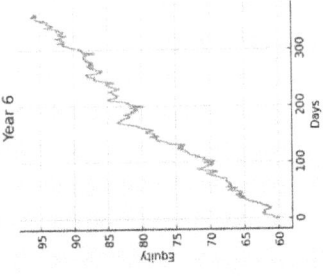

Year 6

You make a mistake, and the market does not punish you. In fact, sometimes, breaking the rules even works in your favour.

Look at stop-losses — something every seasoned trader swears by. In a raging bull market, ignoring your stop can actually lead to better results because most stocks bounce back. This tricks traders into thinking stop-losses are not necessary. "It is not a loss until you sell," they say. That is where they go wrong. They are learning from conditions that will not last. Their trading decisions are based on an environment that is temporary, not the core principles that hold true across all market cycles. The problem? No one knows when conditions will change. And when they do, the traders who built bad habits in an easy market get crushed. At its core, this comes down to discipline. Adapting based on short-term results instead of solid principles is a dangerous game. And most traders play it. Here are some ways they fail to stay disciplined, leading to bigger problems down the road:

1. Tinkering with their stop-loss

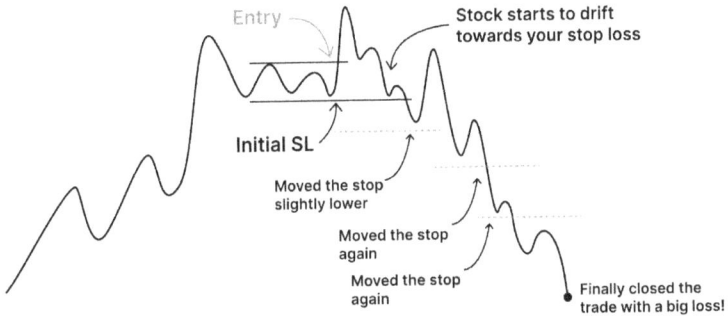

Entry

Stock starts to drift towards your stop loss

Initial SL

Moved the stop slightly lower

Moved the stop again

Moved the stop again

Finally closed the trade with a big loss!

One of the most common mistakes losing traders make — over and over again — is not sticking to their initial stop-loss. It is not that they plan to break their rules. They set their stop at a predetermined level, just like they are supposed to. But as the price starts rushing toward it, their heartbeat picks up. Maybe they start sweating a little — especially if they are holding a big position. And that is when the 'what ifs' start creeping in.

"What if the trade reverses right after I sell?"
"What if this is just a shakeout?"
"What if I am selling at the exact bottom like an idiot?"

Suddenly, moving the stop just a little lower feels like the right move. Then a little more. And then a bit more. Before they know it, they are holding a loss much bigger than they ever intended — too big to close without serious pain.

Now, if you are lucky, you will take a hit big enough to teach you a lesson. That slap on the wrist might keep you from breaking your rules again. But if you are one of the unlucky ones who held on and somehow recovered, I have bad news for you.

Wait — unlucky? Yes, you got that right. If you broke your rules, ignored your stop, and got away with it, you are in trouble. Because now you think maybe it is okay to do this. Maybe holding on to losers is not so bad. Maybe stop-losses do not always need to be followed. That is where it all goes wrong. Once you let yourself believe that discipline is optional, it is only a matter of time before the market proves you dead wrong. And when that day comes, you will not just lose a trade — you will lose big. You already know how that story ends.

2. Not adhering to their entry criteria

One of the biggest mistakes beginners make when trading a profitable system is trying to outsmart it. They think, "What if I get in a little earlier? What if I can predict the signal before it happens?" The logic seems simple — if they can anticipate their system's moves, they will make even more money. This mistake comes from two things:

1. The belief that they can outthink their system.
2. The nagging thought that there is something better out there — some secret strategy that could generate even bigger returns.

But here is the problem: when you step outside the rules of a tested system, you are flying blind. A system you have backtested and studied gives you confidence because you know its strengths, weaknesses, and expected outcomes. Even if it is not the world's best system, it is still better than trading on impulse, chasing short-term noise, or following a half-baked idea.

When you trade on a whim, what do you rely on? You do not know how many losses it can produce, how deep the drawdowns can go, or what kind of returns you can expect if it works. You have no structure—just gut feeling. And gut feeling, over time, is a fast track to disaster. This is how traders get caught in a never-ending cycle—jumping from system to system, chasing "shiny objects," and never sticking with anything long enough to see real results.

It is not wrong to explore new strategies, but there is a right way to do it. Random inputs will always produce random outputs. If you want consistency in your trading results, you need consistency in your process. Tinker too much, and you will not outperform your system—you will sabotage it.

3. Not adhering to their exit criteria

Even experienced traders struggle with sticking to their exit plan. They know discipline leads to better long-term results, but when emotions take over, they often cave to short-term urges—whether it is banking profits too soon or holding on to losses too long.

I have seen traders in deep losses, and I have seen traders sitting on solid gains. Guess who looked more stressed? Surprisingly, the ones with profits. It is human nature— when you are losing, you hope it will turn around. But when you are winning, you fear the market will take it back. Loss aversion kicks in. Studies show that the pain of losing feels twice as strong as the pleasure of winning. So, when traders see a decent profit, their minds start racing: "What if this disappears? What if I do not get another trade like this?" All it takes is a tiny push—maybe a slight pullback or a random tweet—and boom, they hit sell. The worst part is that the moment they exit, regret creeps in. They want back in, but now they are attached to the profits they just locked in. Re-entering feels like risking those gains, so they hesitate, watching from the sidelines as the stock moves higher without them. Sometimes, this behaviour stems from a past trade that went south. Maybe they did hold on once, and it backfired. Now, their subconscious treats every new trade like a ticking time bomb. Even though one trade means nothing in the grand scheme, their mindset shifts into scarcity mode, leading to even more undisciplined decisions down the road.

The solution? Trust your system, not your emotions. The moment fear or greed influences your decisions, you are no longer trading—you are reacting.

4. Trading with too much size

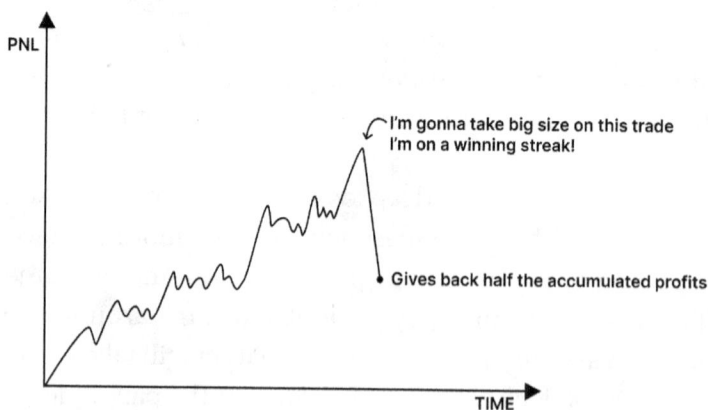

I'm gonna take big size on this trade I'm on a winning streak!

Gives back half the accumulated profits

Proper position sizing can make or break a trader. Used wisely, it fuels long-term growth. Used recklessly, it can end a trading career. Most traders understand this. They know that consistently taking good trades with a reasonable size leads to solid returns over time. But discipline is where things fall apart. After a few wins, overconfidence creeps in. Suddenly, past profits feel like pocket change compared to what they could be making. They crank up their size, dreaming of making in a week what once took a year. This is where disaster strikes. Even the best traders cap their risk per trade, no matter how confident they are because the market does not care about your conviction. A perfect setup, a rock-solid thesis—it all means nothing if a big player decides to dump their shares and you are caught on the wrong side. There was nothing wrong with the trade—it was just probability playing out. But what was wrong was the reckless belief that you were untouchable.

The market is not a place where you impose your will; it is a place where survival comes first. The sooner you accept that, the better your chances of thriving. Focus on staying in the game, not on hitting home runs. Because in the end, the ones who last the longest win.

5. Overtrading

Overtrading is simple—it is trading just for the sake of it, taking setups that do not actually fit your system. The biggest culprit is boredom. Even the best traders fall into this trap occasionally. The problem is, trading is not like a regular job. You are not paid to work—you are paid to wait. The fewer unnecessary trades you take, the better your results.

If you're clicking buttons just to feel productive, you're not trading, you're just making your broker rich.

Think of a cougar hunting. It does not chase every movement in the jungle. It waits. It lets its prey get comfortable before striking at the perfect moment. A trader should do the same. Patience is the real skill here—before the trade and during it. But most people cannot handle the stillness. They crave action, excitement—something happening at all times. The reality is that professional trading is mostly boring. It is long stretches of nothing, punctuated by short bursts of action. What you do in those quiet periods determines your success. Pros understand this. They do not measure results in days but in years. They do not chase daily income; they wait for those rare, high-probability setups that can make up for months of inactivity. The amateur, on the other hand, refuses to accept this truth. He believes money can be made all the time—he just has not figured out how yet. But the market does not care what he believes. It does what it does. And those who impose their expectations on it get punished.

In the end, discipline is not just about making good trades—it is about not making bad ones. Pressing buttons is easy. Not pressing them is the real challenge. The traders who master that are the ones who win.

6. Not being punctual with their trading routine (journaling, planning, etc.)

The market teaches lessons. Your journal makes sure you don't forget them.

It is often said that if you have average intelligence, you can make it in trading. But if you are mentally lazy, no amount of intelligence will save you. Most people think trading is just sitting at a screen, clicking a few buttons, and making or losing money. That is it—just another get-rich-quick gig. But real trading demands far more. The best traders? They work harder than anyone. They are obsessed with understanding the mechanics of the market, refining their edge, and sharpening their discipline. Yet, outsiders see traders as lucky gamblers, messing around with money. That perception usually comes from those who either never traded or failed quickly. In reality, trading takes a brutal work ethic. You need a relentless drive to figure out how this game works, a competitive fire to level up every day, and the hunger to keep learning—even when you think you have "got it." Building a playbook, mastering your system, refining pre- and post-market routines, reviewing watchlists, journaling trades—this is where the real work happens.

Most traders do not fail because they lack intelligence. They fail because they lack discipline. They think they can just show up at 9:15 and start placing trades. But by the time the market opens, the real work should already be done.

7. Closing positions that are in the green to compensate for losses

One of the major mistakes that traders make due to a lack of discipline is trying to close their day in the green by closing positions that are showing some profits in order to compensate for those that stopped them out. This might not seem like a big mistake, but if you are trading a convex strategy — a strategy that takes advantage of asymmetric opportunities by finding low-risk situations — it could be a significant error.

Most gains in such systems come from a small number of trades, and that percentage could be as low as 5–10%. Missing out on or mismanaging those few trades could be detrimental to such a trading system. When traders try to close their day in the green to feel good in the short term, they give up potential long-term gains that could lead to far bigger growth in their trading journey. Succumbing to such behaviour not only lowers the profitability of your system but also lowers your confidence.

You might see some of the positions you exited hastily making big moves, which can lead to further problems like trying to compensate for missing out on those big movers, potentially leading to overtrading. This is a vicious cycle that many traders get into, and it becomes harder and harder to come out the other side victorious. It is better not to allow such behaviours and undisciplined issues to surface in the first place. It takes a lot of discipline to follow your trading plan and not cut trades just because you want to close the day in the green to feel good about yourself. Those who develop this discipline go on to achieve results that most people can only imagine.

Now that we have discussed some of the most common discipline issues that traders face in their journey, it is even more apparent why you need discipline in your trading. So, let us discuss how you can cultivate it in your trading.

DISCIPLINE

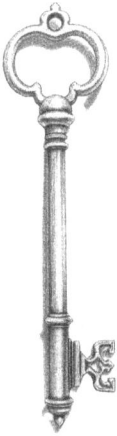

Discipline is the key that unlocks the doors you keep knocking on.

The first thing you need to understand about discipline is what it is not. It is not something that you are born with, and it is not something that only a few special people have and others do not. Then what is it? It is like a muscle—it will not develop on its own, you have to train it. Discipline is basically the bridge between intention and achievement. The first and foremost thing you can do to put yourself on the path that leads to discipline is to instill this belief that there is nothing wrong with you if you are not disciplined—you are not broken, you are perfectly fine. You probably just have not trained this metaphorical muscle we call discipline. The good thing is, you still have a chance. So, let us begin by understanding what are some things you can do to cultivate discipline in your trading.

1. Build discipline outside trading

Many people think trading is separate from the rest of their life. But it is not. As the saying goes, how you do one thing is how you do everything. If you are lazy in daily life, you will be lazy in trading. If you do not pay attention to details outside trading, you will not pay attention to them in the market. Trading is just a reflection of who you are. To be disciplined in trading, you first need to be disciplined in other areas. That could mean staying fit, sticking to good habits, or simply following through on what you say you will do. Most people do not take their goals seriously. They say they will do something but never actually do it. If you do not take action, you will not get results. Ask yourself, 'Do I really want to do this?' If the answer is yes, write down clear steps to get better. For example, if you want to read more books, do not just say, I will read 10 books this year. Instead, decide to read 10 pages every morning at 8 a.m. Make it a part of your routine. If you still do not follow through, the problem might be something deeper. Maybe you do not have a strong reason for doing it.

People need purpose. Without it, you are like a boat drifting in the ocean with no direction. A strong reason (why you are doing something) makes it easier to stay disciplined and take action.

2. Building a vision and an anti-vision

To find your purpose, think about where you want to be in a few years — and just as importantly, where you do not want to be. Clarity on these aspects gives you something to aim for, while an anti-vision helps you avoid paths that lead to failure. Knowing both keeps you motivated.

Start by picturing your ideal future. What does success look like? How do you feel? What kind of life are you living every day? Imagine it in detail. This vision should excite you and push you to take action. Now, think about the future you do not want. What does failure look like? What bad habits or mistakes could lead you there? Be clear about this, so you can avoid it. Once you have both your vision and anti-vision, set clear goals that move you in the right direction. Break them into small steps you can follow daily. This way, every action brings you closer to success and away from failure. In the context of trading, this might mean setting goals such as:

- Dedicating a certain amount of time each day to studying historical winners
- Building a playbook of your best setups
- Analysing your past trades to learn from mistakes
- Practising meditation to maintain a calm and focused mind

Whatever the goals may be, ensure they are specific, measurable, and achievable within a realistic timeframe.

PARADIGM SHIFT

A paradigm is your overall view of the world—a framework that helps you make sense of things. It covers the mental models you use, the beliefs you hold, the options you perceive in different situations, and the decisions you make based on those options. To cultivate discipline, especially in trading, you need a paradigm shift. Start by examining the beliefs and assumptions that define your current behaviours—are

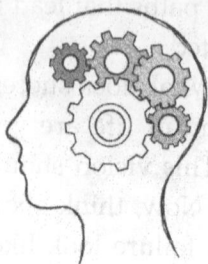

Your trading results are a reflection of your mindset. Upgrade the mindset, upgrade the results.

they serving you well, or are they holding you back? For example, if you believe that you must always be in the market to catch every move, you might find yourself making impulsive trades. On the other hand, a belief that patience pays off could lead you to wait for the right opportunities. Question your assumptions and replace limiting beliefs with empowering ones to attain discipline.

3. The turning point

One way to build discipline and change your habits is by reaching a point where you are so frustrated with your own mistakes that you have to change. For many traders, this moment comes when losses, bad decisions, and stress pile up to the point where they cannot ignore them anymore. It usually happens in stages. First, you notice a pattern — maybe you keep making impulsive trades, ignoring your plan, or overtrading. Then, the emotional toll kicks in. Frustration, regret, and self-doubt start creeping in. You might even wonder if you are cut out for trading at all. At some point, you hit rock bottom. This moment forces you to see reality: what you are doing is not working, and something has to change. That is when a real desire to improve kicks in. The pain of past mistakes pushes you to build better habits and follow a smarter strategy.

It is not an easy process, but if you stick with it and adopt a growth mindset, you can use that pain to turn your trading around for good.

4. Establish clear rules

As mentioned in the earlier chapter, establishing clear rules can help you deal with any emotional issue you are facing in your trading, and discipline is no different. The lack of clear mechanical rules allows you to easily break your rules because you do not have any guard rails in place. When you do not have clarity about your trading rules, you have no way of telling when you are deviating from your system, and that certainly does not help to build discipline.

Clear rules provide a benchmark against which you can measure your performance. When you follow a well-defined trading plan, you can objectively analyse your trades and identify areas for improvement. This feedback loop is essential for building discipline, as it allows you to learn from your experiences and progressively refine your trading system. Over time, the practice of adhering to clear rules will become second nature, fostering a disciplined mindset that is essential for long-term success in trading.

Remember, discipline and clarity go hand in hand.

5. Second-order thinking

Second-order thinking is a great tool for building discipline and I have not seen many people talk about it. Most people, when making decisions, only consider the immediate consequences of those decisions. However, decisions often have ripple effects that extend beyond the immediate outcome. Second-order thinking involves looking beyond these direct consequences to consider the indirect ones as

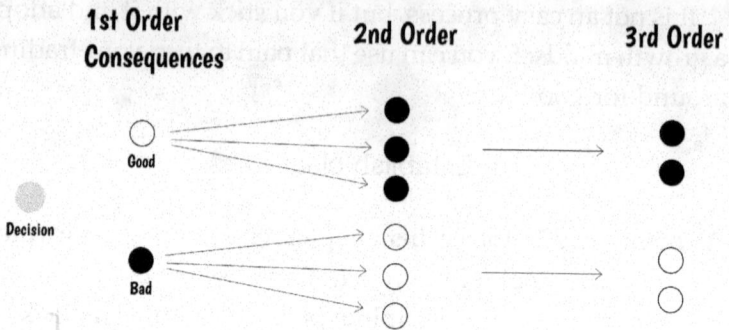

well, which may impact you far into the future. By learning and understanding more about second-order thinking, you can develop a mindset that anticipates and prepares for these indirect effects. This way of thinking is not just about recognising that each decision has a second-order effect, but also understanding that each of these second-order effects can lead to further second-order effects of their own, creating a chain reaction. This is similar to what is famously known as the butterfly effect, where a small decision can lead to big changes over time, whether positive or negative, depending on the initial choice. Incorporating second-order thinking into your decision-making process helps you develop a habit of thorough analysis and foresight. This not only improves the quality of your decisions but also strengthens your overall discipline. If you are consistent with this approach you can become more adept at anticipating potential outcomes and preparing for them, leading to more controlled and deliberate actions. This level of strategic thinking is essential for maintaining discipline in all aspects of life, particularly in trading, where the ability to foresee and manage potential risks is of greatest importance. For example, when you are about to make a selling decision and you see that you are not adhering to your overall plan, ask yourself what the second-order effects of this decision will be. For example, you might be right this time and save yourself some money by exiting the trade before even your system produces a sell signal, but the second-order effect of this is going to be that you will assume it is okay to break your rules sometimes, and it pays to be ahead of your system. This decision could create its own second-order effects down the line, such as gradually eroding your discipline and consistency. Over time, you might find yourself making more decisions based on gut feelings rather than following your established trading system. This habit can lead to increased emotional trading, where most of your decisions are driven by fear or greed rather than rational analysis.

The cumulative impact of these undisciplined decisions can be quite destructive for your overall trading performance. Moreover, frequently deviating from your plan could make you lose the ability to assess the effectiveness of your trading strategy. If you constantly second-guess your system and making ad-hoc decisions, it becomes challenging to identify whether the strategy itself needs adjustments or if the problem lies in your lack of adherence to it. This confusion can lead to unnecessary changes in your trading approach, further complicating your efforts to build and maintain discipline.

6. Find a Trading Buddy

We all assume that being your own boss might be the best feeling in the world, but it also comes with its own set of problems. Trading is a lonely business; you have no one to report to, and whether you do your homework or not is your choice alone.

No one is going to nudge you if you do not perform well for a while, and no one is going to cheer for you (other than your close ones, but they probably do not understand what is going on behind the scenes). All in all, you are on your own. This might be the one thing stopping you from reaching your full potential.

A trading buddy could solve this problem, as they can provide the much-needed accountability and support that often gets lost when you are working alone. Having a trading buddy means you have someone to share your goals with, discuss strategies, and review each other's trades. This partnership can help you stay disciplined because you are no longer operating in isolation. When you know someone else is counting on you and will hold you accountable for your trading decisions, it becomes easier to stick to your trading plan and avoid impulsive decisions. Such a mutual support system can help you cultivate a disciplined approach to trading, where both of you strive to achieve consistent and sustainable results.

CHAPTER SUMMARY

DISCIPLINE IN TRADING

DISCIPLINE IS KEY

BULL MARKETS CAN DECEIVE

COMMON MISTAKES

THE PROBLEM WITH WHAT IF

TRADING REQUIRES HARD WORK

SOFT EDGE WITH DISCIPLINE

HARD EDGE FAILS WITHOUT DISCIPLINE

EASY PROFITS IN BULL MARKETS LEAD TO UNDISCIPLINED HABITS, PUNISHED IN CHALLENGING MARKETS

TINKERING WITH STOP LOSSES DEVIATING FROM ENTRY/EXIT CRITERIA TRADING WITH EXCESSIVE SIZE OVERTRADING

WHAT IF leads to EMOTIONAL DECISIONS and MOVING STOP LOSSES BIGGER LOSSES

CONSISTENT EFFORT IN PLANNING, JOURNALING, AND STRONG WORK ETHIC TO UNDERSTAND MARKET

HARD WORK

AVOID EASY PROFITS

CONSISTENCY

10

FLEXIBILITY AND ADAPTABILITY: THE TRAITS OF WINNING TRADERS

"It is not the strongest or the most intelligent who will survive but those who can best manage change."

—Charles Darwin

Traders have different opinions about flexibility in trading. Some believe you should always follow a fixed set of rules, considering discipline and consistency as the keys to success. Others argue that being flexible and adjusting to market conditions is more important. So, who is right? The truth is, there is no single right way to trade.

Trading is not an exact science—it is more like an art. What matters most is finding what works for *you*, rather than copying what others do. Over time, your understanding of flexibility and adaptability will change. You will face different challenges, learn new lessons, and adjust your strategies along the way. This process is not a straight path. Most traders go through different phases. At first, they trade with complete freedom, making decisions on the spot. Then, they shift to strict rules, thinking structure will bring better results. Eventually, they find a balance—using both rules and flexibility to improve their trading.

These phases are:

Phase 1: Chaotic discretionary phase

Pros:

- ✔ Freedom to trade however you want
- ✔ Excitement and thrill of the market
- ✔ No rigid rules, fully flexible
- ✔ Big wins can happen

Cons:

- ✖ No consistency in results
- ✖ Emotional trading
- ✖ No risk management
- ✖ Overtrading

When people start trading, they are often drawn to the freedom it offers. The idea of making their own decisions—without anyone telling them what to do—feels exciting, especially if they have come from jobs with strict rules. This craving for independence leads to what I call the *chaotic discretionary phase*. In this phase, traders rely on gut feelings, intuition, or random bits of information to make trades. There is no real strategy or plan, so their results swing wildly between profits and losses. Emotions like fear, greed, and excitement take over, making their trading unpredictable. Many traders at this stage resist rules because they think too much structure will take away the thrill of trading. They believe trusting their instincts is the best way to go. But over time, the excitement turns into frustration. Without a clear system, their results stay inconsistent, and making steady profits feels impossible. Eventually, they realise they need more structure and predictability, which leads them to the next phase.

Phase 2: Structured mechanical phase

Pros:

- ✅ Clear rules = Less emotional trading
- ✅ Consistent execution
- ✅ Backtested strategies for confidence
- ✅ Strong risk management

Cons:

- ❌ Too rigid, might not adapt to new conditions
- ❌ Over-reliance on systems
- ❌ Lacking creativity, feels robotic
- ❌ Struggles when market changes

After going through the chaos of the first phase, traders realise they need more structure to make consistent profits. This leads them to the *structured mechanical phase*. Here, they follow strict rules and systems to guide their trades. The goal is to remove emotions from their decisions and stick to a clear plan. In this phase, discipline is everything. Traders spend a lot of time backtesting strategies to make sure they work over time. They want their trading to be as systematic as possible, so they do not fall into emotional trading again.

For many, this phase feels like a breakthrough. After all the ups and downs of the previous phase, having a rules-based approach brings a sense of control and stability. But the market is always changing, and rigid systems do not always hold up when new conditions appear. Eventually, traders see the need for more flexibility, which leads them to the final phase.

Phase 3: Balanced adaptive phase

In the final phase, traders find a balance between structure and flexibility. They take what they have learned from

Pros:

- ✅ Combines structure and flexibility
- ✅ Adapts to different market conditions
- ✅ Disciplined yet creative
- ✅ Long-term sustainable success

Cons:

- ✖ Takes years of experience to reach this level
- ✖ Requires deep market understanding
- ✖ Harder to teach, as it blends intuition with rules

both the chaotic and strict rule-based phases, and develop a trading style that is both disciplined and adaptable. This is the *balanced adaptive phase*. Traders still follow rules and strategies, but they also make adjustments based on real-time market conditions. They understand that no single system works all the time, so they stay open to adapting when needed. This phase is about knowing when to stick to a plan and when to be flexible.

By this stage, traders are usually more experienced and confident. They have a strong understanding of both the markets and themselves. They know when to strictly follow their plan and when to make adjustments. This balanced approach helps them trade more effectively, leading to consistent and sustainable success.

THE IMPORTANCE OF FLEXIBILITY AND ADAPTABILITY IN TRADING

Markets are always changing. They react to things like economic events, politics, new technology, and shifts in investor mood. What worked yesterday might not work today, and what works today may fail tomorrow. That is why being able to adapt is not just useful—it is necessary for long-term success.

Traders who stick to one strategy no matter what, risk being left behind when the market shifts. But those who can adjust based on new information or changing conditions have a much better chance of staying ahead. Being flexible helps traders spot new opportunities as they come up. It also allows them to change course when a strategy stops working instead of holding on to a losing plan out of fear or stubbornness.

In the end, adaptability is not just a nice skill to have — it is a real advantage in the market.

THE EVOLUTIONARY PSYCHOLOGY BEHIND RESISTANCE TO CHANGE

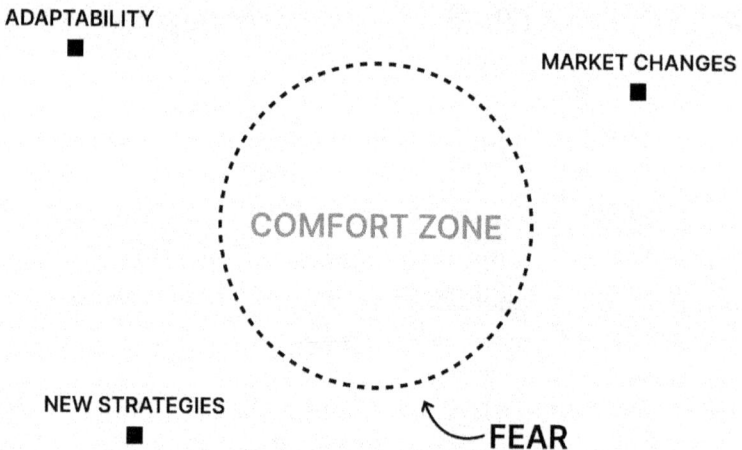

ADAPTABILITY
■

MARKET CHANGES
■

COMFORT ZONE

NEW STRATEGIES
■

⌐FEAR

Why do so many traders struggle with flexibility, even when they know it is important? A big part of the answer comes from human psychology. As humans, we naturally seek comfort and avoid uncertainty. In early human history, sticking to familiar routines and avoiding the unknown often meant a better chance of survival. Our brains are wired to recognise patterns and rely on them, which helped reduce risks in unpredictable environments. In trading, this instinct can make it hard to adapt. Traders often get attached to a strategy simply because it worked in the past. The brain, which wants the safety of the familiar, resists change—even when market conditions are clearly shifting.

Fear of the unknown also plays a role. Dropping a trusted strategy for something untested can feel risky, triggering anxiety and hesitation. This fear can cause traders to hold on to losing strategies longer than they should, just because changing feels even scarier.

But once traders understand these psychological barriers, they can start working through them. The first step is awareness—recognising when the fear of change or habit is affecting decisions. From there, they can train themselves to be more adaptable, staying open to new information and adjusting when needed.

LEARNING TO ADAPT: PRACTICAL STEPS FOR TRADERS

So, how can traders cultivate flexibility and adaptability in their approach?

1. Continuous learning

One of the best ways to become more adaptable is to keep learning. Markets always change, and your knowledge should too. Stay updated on market trends, new strategies, and emerging technologies. Watch webinars, read books, and follow experienced traders to keep improving your skills. The more you learn, the easier it becomes to adjust and stay ahead.

2. Embracing small changes

Being adaptable does not mean you have to make big changes all at once. Start small. Try adjusting your entry or exit points, or test a new indicator in your analysis. Making gradual changes helps you become more flexible without feeling overwhelmed. Over time, these small tweaks add up and make it easier to adapt when needed.

3. Flexibility in strategy, rigidity in risk management

Being flexible with your strategy — like adjusting entry and exit points or trying different trailing techniques — can improve your edge. This is an important distinction every trader needs to understand.

But some things should never change. Risk management is one of them. No matter how adaptable you are, your risk management rules should stay firm. This means always using stop-losses, sticking to proper position sizing, and following your risk-reward ratios. These rules protect your capital, and being too flexible with them can lead to big losses.

4. Developing a balanced adaptive approach

As you gain experience, work on finding a balance between structure and flexibility. Have a clear trading plan with set rules, but also stay open to adjustments when the market changes.

Over time, this approach will help you trade more effectively — taking advantage of opportunities while keeping risks under control.

THE ONGOING JOURNEY OF ADAPTABILITY

In the end, there is no single right way to trade. It is a personal journey, and every trader has to figure out what works best for them. The key is to keep learning, adapting, and finding a balance that fits your style and goals. Flexibility and adaptability are crucial, but each trader's path will be different. You cannot just skip ahead to the balanced adaptive phase, no matter how much you want to. The only way to get there is by going through the struggles of the first two phases. Each phase teaches important lessons that help you build the skills and experience needed to find balance.

The first phase shows you the risks of trading based purely on emotion and intuition. It is messy and unpredictable, but it is an essential step in understanding why structure is important.

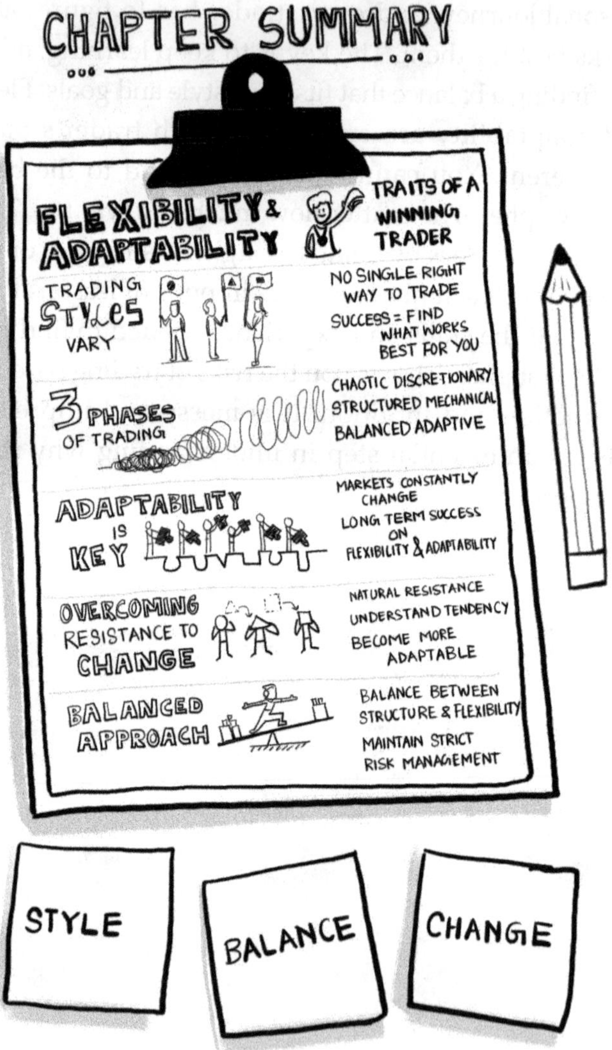
CHAPTER SUMMARY
FLEXIBILITY & ADAPTABILITY
TRAITS OF A WINNING TRADER
TRADING STYLES VARY
NO SINGLE RIGHT WAY TO TRADE
SUCCESS = FIND WHAT WORKS BEST FOR YOU
3 PHASES OF TRADING
CHAOTIC DISCRETIONARY
STRUCTURED MECHANICAL
BALANCED ADAPTIVE
ADAPTABILITY IS KEY
MARKETS CONSTANTLY CHANGE
LONG TERM SUCCESS ON FLEXIBILITY & ADAPTABILITY
OVERCOMING RESISTANCE TO CHANGE
NATURAL RESISTANCE
UNDERSTAND TENDENCY
BECOME MORE ADAPTABLE
BALANCED APPROACH
BALANCE BETWEEN STRUCTURE & FLEXIBILITY
MAINTAIN STRICT RISK MANAGEMENT
STYLE
BALANCE
CHANGE

11

STAYING FOCUSED AND AVOIDING DISTRACTIONS

"A wealth of information creates a poverty of attention."
— Herbert A. Simon

L et me start this chapter with a story about a friend of mine who was a trader. He almost lost his edge because he got too distracted from his trading.

I will not reveal his real name, so let us call him Ricky. Ricky and I have been friends since we started trading. We met online, and since we were both complete beginners trying to figure things out, we would discuss everything — trading ideas, technical tools, strategies, and even the psychological side of trading. It was an exciting time. We were both at the same stage, with no real edge in the market, just learning as we went. At this stage, networking really helps. The more traders you meet, the more styles and strategies you learn about. It is a great way to speed up your growth.

After a few quarters, both of us had finally developed an edge. We had solid strategies and knew what worked for us. We were ready to take things to the next level. Up until this point, all the networking and social media had been helpful—it expanded our knowledge and played a big role in our progress.

But then Ricky ran into a problem—information overload. The very thing that had helped us grow—constant discussions, trade ideas, and staying updated—was now starting to work against us. We had discord groups where we shared market updates, new trade setups, and opinions. This was great when we were still learning, but it started becoming a distraction—especially for Ricky.

I handled it better for some reason, but it started affecting everything for him. Ricky could not stick to his plan. If he saw an experienced trader post a negative view on one of his trades, he would either get frustrated or make an impulsive exit. The same thing happened with his entries and risk

management—his entire system fell apart because he was paying too much attention to other people's opinions. The result? His performance took a huge hit. Instead of making the 50% return that his system should have delivered over a few months, he ended up making just 8%—an 80% underperformance—all because of decision paralysis.

You see, information by itself is not good or bad. It is just a tool. When you do not have a trading system, the more you learn, the better. But once you have a system that works over the long term, too much information can hurt you. Constantly looking at what other traders are doing or following every market update (unless it is part of your system) will only make things worse.

Ricky was not the only one who faced this problem. One of the greatest traders of all time, Nicolas Darvas, went through the same thing. Darvas built a fortune using his unique trading strategy. He travelled the world, trading based on price movements while staying away from market noise. But when he returned to the financial hubs and started paying attention to news, expert opinions, and constant updates, his trading suffered. He began second-guessing his trades, hesitating when he should have acted, and making impulsive moves when he should have stayed patient. His once-successful strategy fell apart, and he lost a big chunk of his capital. The very thing that made him successful— his ability to focus—was destroyed by information overload.

The lesson here is simple: too much information can be just as dangerous as too little. As a trader, your biggest challenge is filtering out the noise and staying focused on what actually matters—your system and the principles that drive it.

Here are a few problems that traders who are exposed to too much information struggle with.

1. Analysis paralysis

How a pro trader executes his trades:

System produces ————————→ Initiates position
a buy signal

How an amateur trader executes his trades:

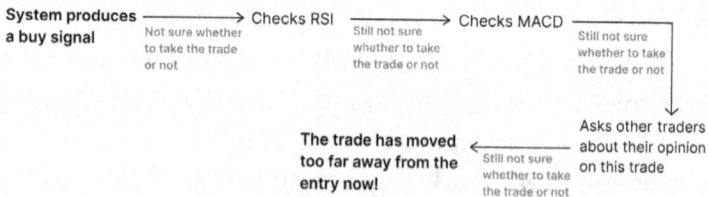

System produces ————————→ Checks RSI ————————→ Checks MACD ————— Still not sure
a buy signal   Not sure whether   Still not sure   whether to take
               to take the trade   whether to take   the trade or not
               or not   the trade or not

                                                              Asks other traders
                         The trade has moved ←——————————— about their opinion
                         too far away from the   Still not sure   on this trade
                         entry now!   whether to take
                                                 the trade or not

Have you ever meticulously planned a trade—checked every detail, gone through your checklist, and confirmed that this was a five-star setup according to your system— only to back out at the last moment? Almost instantly, you know you have made a mistake. You let go of a great trade, and you beat yourself up over it. Most traders assume this happens because they lack discipline or there is something wrong with their mindset. But that is not really the case. More often than not, traders miss out on these setups due to analysis paralysis—a direct result of being overloaded with too much information.

Look at any struggling trader, and you will notice a pattern. They are in every group chat and discord server discussing the market. They keep news channels on throughout the trading session. And before they even start their day, they will check their favourite trading guru's social media handle, looking for insights. This constant influx of information—starting from the moment you wake up until you go to bed—is ruining your trading.

Think about it. If you already have a system that works, what is the point of constantly searching for more information? Is it really improving your trading in any meaningful way? Probably not. The real reason you keep chasing more information is comfort. You want reassurance. If other traders agree with your market view, you feel more confident, like your trade has a better chance of working out. But that is an illusion. You could have all the conviction in the world, and the trade could still fail. So why keep looking for more confirmation?

Once you understand this, you start cutting out the noise. You begin to see how all these discussion groups, news channels, and opinions do not help you—they make you more vulnerable to impulsive decisions. Eliminating this excess information will not just improve your trading results; it will free up mental space, making you a more confident and decisive trader.

2. Fear of missing out

We talked about FOMO in the second chapter when we discussed the various types of fear that traders face every single trading day. It is important to bring it up again here because it is closely linked to why traders constantly feel distracted and unable to focus. It is normal to want to stay informed and not miss out on something important. In trading, this tendency gets amplified because there is money on the line. Traders worry that if they are not tuned in to every bit of news or every expert opinion, they might miss something crucial—something that could make or break their trade. This fear drives them to constantly check news feeds, social media, and group chats. But instead of helping, it does the opposite. It leads to doubt, confusion, and second-guessing. A trader might see someone on X (formerly Twitter) posting an opinion that contradicts their own analysis, and suddenly, they feel uncertain about their trade. They start questioning themselves, hesitating when they should act or changing their plan at the last minute. This kind of distraction often leads to overtrading—taking unnecessary trades based on incomplete or misleading information. Instead of following their system, they chase ideas, trying to keep up with every new piece of data.

Ricky went through the same thing. Even though he had a solid strategy, he got caught up in the endless stream of opinions and market updates. He spent more time reacting to what others were saying than focusing on his own plan. This did not just impact his trading results—it took a toll on his confidence and mental state. Instead of feeling in control, he felt lost in a flood of information.

The key takeaway here is simple: more information does not always mean better decisions. In fact, too much information can cloud your judgment and lead to analysis paralysis. The goal is to find a balance—having enough information to make informed decisions, but not so much that it overwhelms you. This means being selective about the information you consume, setting specific times to check the news, and most importantly, trusting your own strategy and analysis.

3. Cognitive overload

Too much information is not just bad for your trading—it is bad for you mentally and physically. When you are constantly bombarded with data, your brain gets exhausted. This mental fatigue can leave you feeling stressed, overwhelmed, and unable to focus. Even simple decisions start to feel difficult.

Think about it—when you try to track every market update, every tweet from a trading guru, and every opinion from a group chat, your mind is processing too many pieces of information at the same. This does not just hurt your trading performance; it drains your overall well-being.

Then there is the comparison trap. When you constantly see other traders' profits, opinions, and trade setups, it is easy to start doubting yourself. Thoughts like, 'Why am I not making as much money as they are?' or 'What am I doing wrong?' creep in. This kind of thinking kills confidence. Instead of focusing on your own progress, you get caught up in what others are doing. You might even start feeling like a failure—even if you are making steady gains—just because someone else is posting bigger wins. This negativity does not just affect your trading; it seeps into other areas of your life, impacting your overall happiness and mindset.

That is why as a trader, your goal should be to cut out the noise. Anything that does not add value to your trading or your life needs to go. Focus only on what truly matters.

Now that we have covered what distracts traders and hurts their focus, let us dive into some practical ways to stay sharp and avoid these pitfalls.

1. Create a morning routine for your trading

One of the biggest things that has helped me improve my trading over the years is having a fixed morning routine. A trader's morning routine is about structuring your time from the moment you wake up until you sit at your desk to start trading. The first, most important part of this routine is your daily ritual. I do mine right after waking up. Most people start their day by grabbing their phone first thing in the morning. It seems harmless, but it is probably one of the biggest reasons you are struggling — not just in trading, but in life. Think about it. The moment you check social media, the news, or even your emails, you are filling your mind with noise — information that is neither useful nor necessary. Everything you see online is designed to hijack your attention because attention is valuable. Companies want to sell you something. They want to sell you stories, sell you dreams — everyone is selling something. So do yourself a favour: do not check your phone first thing in the morning. You can set a specific time for it later — we will get to that.

Now, let us talk about what you should do in your morning ritual. But before that, you need to understand why we are doing this in the first place. The "I" in you — the person you think you are — is just a collection of thoughts. The more you entertain a thought, the stronger it becomes. This is how habits are built. The more you repeat something to yourself, the more likely it is to become your reality. Others can shape your beliefs too — if you let them. So it is important to set your own beliefs. That is why we do this morning ritual. The goal is simple: spark feelings of optimism and self-belief. They give you the energy and confidence to take action. And you can create these feelings in different ways. You can think back to times when you set your mind to something and succeeded. How did it feel in those moments? You can focus on gratitude—no matter how tough life is, there is always something to be grateful for.

When you do this, you are training your mind to start the day on a positive note. For a trader, that is huge. Trading is not just about charts and setups—it is a mental game too. The way you start your day impacts how you trade. Once you are done with your morning ritual, the next step is getting ready for the day. After that comes another key part of your routine: your pre-market plan. A pre-market plan can include a lot of things, but one of the most powerful tools is a mental script—a simple, structured way to remind yourself what to focus on throughout the day. Athletes use these habits all the time to stay sharp under pressure, and traders can benefit from them too. It looks something like this:

Morning Ritual Script "P.R.O.M.P.T."

Prepare   Set up charts and other tools.

Review   Go over the previous day's trades and notes.

Observe   Watch market conditions and key levels.

Mental Check   Ensure you're mentally ready.

Plan   Confirm your strategy and set clear objectives.

Trust   Have faith in your preparation and strategy.

You can create your own checklist of things that matter most to your trading. Since trading is a personal journey, the solutions you come up with for yourself will often be the most effective. By adding these mental scripts to your routine, you can sharpen your focus, become better at decision-making, and improve your overall performance. Think of these as quick reminders to keep you aligned with your plan—just like athletes who use pre-game routines to stay locked in.

The next step is reviewing your trading plan for the day. Most traders prepare their plan the night before, but by morning, it is easy to forget key details. That is why it is important to revisit it before the market opens. Take a few minutes to go over your open positions and potential trade setups. This reinforces your plan and ensures you are mentally ready to execute it without second-guessing.

2. Choose your ideals carefully

One mistake almost every trader makes in the beginning is not being selective about who they learn from. Most of us just take people at their word—if someone claims they have made money trading, we assume it must be true without even questioning their methods or results. That is why you see traders with massive followings on social media who have nothing to show in their own trading accounts. It is all just smoke and mirrors. As a trader, you need to recognise this. Most of what you see online is a highlight reel. You get the winning trades, the flashy profits—but never the full picture. That is why it is crucial to curate your feed carefully and only follow people who genuinely add value to your growth. Before you take someone's advice, do some digging. Check their track record. See if they have any verifiable success. Look at their past trades. A good trader with real insights will not need to hide anything. They will often have a transparent history — whether that is through consistently sharing their performance, explaining their strategy in detail, or simply approaching the market with logic and experience.

Also, be wary of those who only talk about their wins and never their losses. Any real trader knows losses are part of the game, and the best ones are not afraid to acknowledge them because there is always something to learn. If someone is just showing off their best trades, chances are, they are not being completely honest.

At the end of the day, your goal is not to blindly copy someone else's trades — it is to sharpen your own skills. Use what you learn to refine your strategies and develop your own edge. Learning from others is important, but real success comes from your ability to think and adapt for yourself.

3. Distraction could take many forms

We have already talked about how social media and mainstream media are designed to hijack your attention, leaving you drained and unfocused. But distractions do not stop there — especially in trading. One of the biggest ways traders get sidetracked is by doing things that were never part of their plan in the first place. It happens in small ways. Maybe you start checking a time frame you do not usually trade. You see some price fluctuations, and suddenly, you are tempted to close your trade early — even though nothing has changed in your original setup. This is a common mistake.

Prices will always move in different ways across different time frames, but that does not mean every move is relevant to your system. This is where understanding your circle of competence becomes crucial. It is the area where you have the most knowledge and expertise. In trading, it means sticking to the strategies, time frames, and markets you actually understand. The moment you step outside familiar territory, you expose yourself to unnecessary risks and distractions.

Warren Buffett is a huge advocate of this concept. He has always said that one of the biggest keys to his success is knowing exactly what he understands — and, more importantly, what he does not. In the early days of his career, he experimented with all sorts of investments, from commodities to tech stocks. But he quickly realised that his best returns came from businesses he truly understood — like insurance, banking, and consumer goods. By focusing on those, he avoided unnecessary risks and maximised his edge. The same logic applies to trading. If you have a system that works for you, stick to it. Just because there is hype around a new strategy or asset class does not mean you need to dive in.

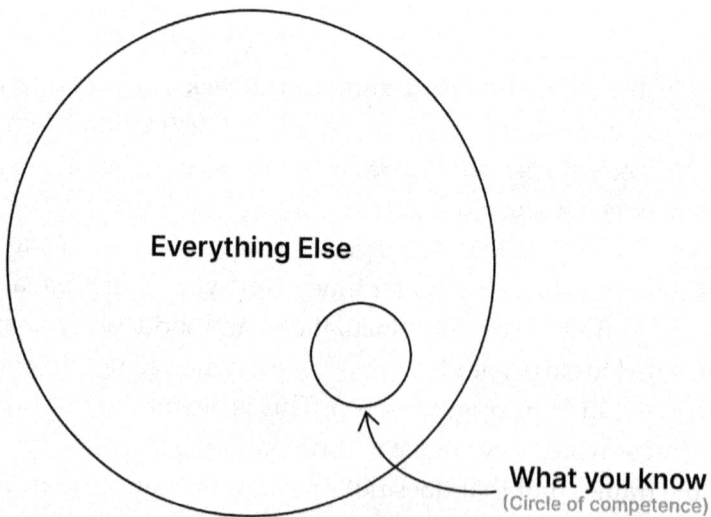

Everything Else

What you know
(Circle of competence)

The more you chase what you do not fully understand, the more mistakes you will make.

4. Keep a pre-trade journal

Keeping a trading journal is one of the best ways to improve and we have discussed it earlier in the book. But there is one more way to use it that most traders are not aware of. Instead of just maintaining a post-trade journal where you document trades after they happen, I have found that a pre-trade journal is even more valuable. A pre-trade journal is exactly what it sounds like—a record of your thoughts, plans, and strategies before you enter any trades. This simple habit can make a massive difference in your trading performance. Before the market opens, I take a few minutes to note down my market outlook, the setups I am following, and the specific trades I will consider for the day. Doing this forces me to think ahead rather than just reacting to price movements in the heat of the moment. This approach brings clarity. When you write down your plan in advance, you do not just trade based on emotions or impulses—you are following a structured, well-thought-out process. Over time, this makes you a more disciplined and confident trader.

Here is what a typical entry in my pre-trade journal might include:

1. I start with an overview of the market conditions. Is it a bullish, bearish, or sideways market? Are there any significant news events or economic data releases that could impact the market today?
2. Next, I list the potential trades I will be watching for the day. This includes notes on why they are on my watchlist—maybe they have strong momentum, a specific pattern, or some news catalyst.
3. After that, I outline the setups I am looking for, for each ticker in my watchlist. This would include specific

price levels or things that would make it a good setup, I also note my entry and exit points and any risk management strategies I plan to use.

4.   Then I take a moment to reflect on my mental state. Do I feel calm and focused, or am I distracted or stressed about something other than trading? This helps me stay aware of any potential emotional biases that could affect my trading.

5.   Finally, I set some goals for the day. These could be performance-based, like sticking to my trading plan or process-based, like not overtrading and maintaining discipline.

The reason I advocate for a pre-trade journal is because of the immense benefits it offers. Here are a few:

1. Clarity and focus

Writing down your plans and strategies helps you clear up your thoughts and focus on what really matters. It reduces the likelihood of making impulsive decisions based on emotions or distractions.

2. Accountability

A pre-trade journal holds you accountable to your plan. When you write down your setups and strategies, you are more likely to stick to them.

3. Preparation

By thinking through potential scenarios and writing them down, you are better prepared for trading. You do not get caught off guard by market movements because you have already considered various possibilities.

4. Self-Awareness

Reflecting on your mental state and emotions before trading helps you become more self-aware. This can prevent emotional trading and help you stay disciplined.

Using a pre-trade journal has transformed my trading, and I believe it can do the same for you. It is a simple practice that requires a bit of time and discipline but pays off immensely in terms of clarity, focus, and overall trading performance. So give it a try, and see how it can help you become a better trader.

5. Make the most of downtime

Nothing happening in the market? Good. Now you have time to get better.

No strategy generates trades all the time. There will always be periods when the market slows down, and there is nothing to do. This is when traders are most vulnerable to distractions — chasing random trades, tweaking strategies unnecessarily, or switching to a completely different system just because something else seems to be working. That is a big mistake. Instead of letting boredom push you into poor decisions, use this downtime productively. One of the best ways to do this is by reading. A good book can offer fresh insights and sharpen your understanding of the markets. Classics like

Reminiscences of a Stock Operator by Edwin Lefèvre provide timeless trading wisdom, while *Atomic Habits* by James Clear helps you build the discipline necessary for success. One of my recent favourites is *Clear Thinking* by Shane Parrish — it is a great read if you want to improve the way you process information and make decisions.

Another smart way to use slow market periods is by refining your trading arsenal. I often spend these downtimes backtesting strategies on historical data to improve my playbook. If you are unfamiliar with the concept of a playbook, it is essentially a collection of trading setups that you have tested and refined over time.

It acts as your personal guide for navigating different market conditions, helping you stay systematic instead of trading impulsively. A well-structured playbook includes clear descriptions of your best setups, ideal entry and exit points, and examples of past trades that worked well. It is like having a cheat sheet that keeps you focused on high-probability trades while filtering out the noise.

By finding productive ways to spend market lulls — whether it is reading, refining your strategies, working on your mindset, or even taking care of your health — you set yourself up for long-term success. Instead of wasting energy on distractions, you will be sharpening the skills that actually matter, making you a more resilient and well-rounded trader.

CHAPTER SUMMARY

STAYING FOCUSSED AND AVOIDING DISTRACTIONS

INFORMATION OVERLOAD HURTS TRADING

SOCIAL MEDIA, GROUPS DISTRACT TRADERS

POOR DECISIONS

ANALYSIS PHRALYSIS AND FOMO

OVER ANALYSIS

FEAR OF MISSING OUT

IMPULSIVE ACTIONS

COGNITIVE OVERLOAD IMPACTS MENTAL HEALTH

CONSTANT INFORMATION INTAKE

MENTAL FATIGUE

STRESS

NEGATIVE SELF COMPARISON

MORNING ROUTINE IS CRUCIAL

MENTAL RITUAL

PRE-MARKET PLANNING

IMPROVE FOCUS AND TRADING PERFORMANCE

CAREFULLY SELECT INFLUENCES

CHOOSE RIGHT PEOPLE TO LEARN

INFORMATION OVERLOAD

ROUTINE

INFLUENCES

12

THE SYSTEM'S EDGE: HOW CONSISTENCY TRANSFORMS TRADING

"Do not let what you cannot do interfere with what you can do."
— John Wooden

One of the biggest responsibilities you take on as a trader is sticking to a system. It sounds simple—if you have built your strategy on a solid foundation and backtested it properly, there is no reason to abandon it, right? But in reality, this is where many traders struggle. They find a strategy, define their rules, turn it into a system, and start trading. Then, after just a few losses, they either ditch it entirely or start making unnecessary changes.

Here is what really happens: traders hit a small drawdown, panic, and assume their system is flawed. Instead of letting probabilities play out, they jump to a new system, thinking that is the solution. But is it? Many traders fall into this cycle of system-hopping. They see others using similar strategies successfully and wonder why they are not getting the same results. The truth is, most failed traders do not give their systems enough time to work. They abandon them too soon, never allowing the edge to play out over a large enough sample size. More often than not, the issue is not the system—it is how traders perceive it. Here are a few reasons why sticking to a system is harder than it seems:

1. Not having a system that fits with the natural tendencies of a trader

The right system feels natural, like a puzzle piece snapping into place. Force the wrong one, and it just won't fit.

We have already explored this in previous chapters—building a system that fits your personality is crucial. If your system does not align with your lifestyle, habits, and mental makeup, you are more likely to abandon it sooner or later. That is just how the law of least resistance works. When something does not feel natural, following through becomes an uphill battle. A common phrase thrown around in trading circles is, "trading is hard." But is it really? I do not think so. Trading is not inherently difficult—we just make it difficult by not understanding market behaviour, not knowing ourselves, and forcing ourselves into systems that do not match how we think and operate.

Another mistake traders make is blindly copying others. Learning from successful traders is valuable, no doubt. But crowd mentality rarely works in your favour. The market rewards those who think independently. To succeed, you need to develop your own insights, trust your instincts, and build a system that reflects your strengths. You do not need constant validation from other traders. In fact, if you want to be truly elite in this game, you have to break free from that mindset. Break the shackles you have put on yourself just because someone else said so. A system is only as good as your ability to stick with it. And the truth is that no system works all the time. The market is unpredictable, and even the best strategies go through rough patches. Many traders abandon their systems the moment they hit a drawdown, not realising that every system has losing streaks.

2. Not accepting drawdowns as the cost of participating in this business

Progress is never a straight line.
The dips are just part of the climb.

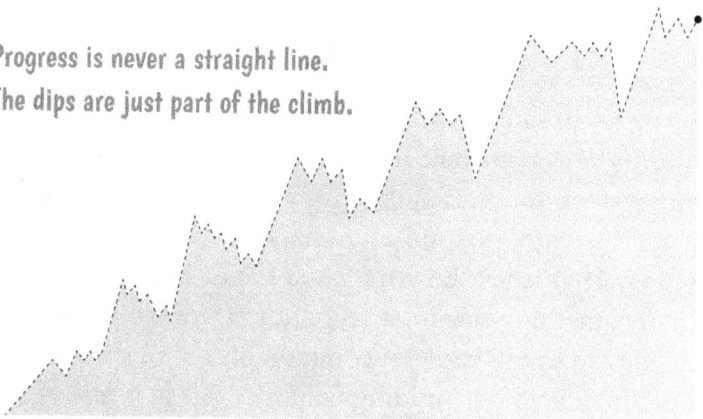

No matter how great your system is, drawdowns are inevitable. But they are not a flaw—they are a feature. Think of trading like a road trip to a beautiful destination. Along the way, you will hit traffic, detours, or rough patches. These slow you down, but they do not stop you from reaching your goal. You do not abandon the journey just because the road is not always smooth, right? Drawdowns in trading are the same. They are the stretches where your trades are not working, and your account balance takes a hit. But this is completely normal. It is just the price of doing business in the markets.

At the core of drawdowns is something called variance. It is what causes results to fluctuate. Imagine rolling a pair of dice — sometimes you will get a high number, sometimes a low one. But over many rolls, you get a mix of both. That is variance at work. Trading operates the same way. Even with a solid strategy, your wins and losses will be spread out over time. Some losing streaks are just part of the game, not a sign that your system is broken.

The biggest mistake traders make is treating drawdowns as a problem to fix. But successful traders understand that these periods are a natural part of trading. What matters is how you manage them. If you accept drawdowns as part of the process, you will be less likely to panic and abandon your strategy when things are not going well. Instead, you will stay focused on the bigger picture — managing risk, sticking to your plan, and letting probabilities play out over time. So, the takeaway is simple: embrace drawdowns. They are just part of the game. The key is to stay disciplined, ride them out, and trust your system. With patience and persistence, the rewards will come.

3. Short-term mindset

Short-term thinking is one of the biggest barriers to reaching your potential. It is when you have two options — one with an immediate reward and one with a bigger reward that requires patience — and you choose the quick win. That is the problem. We are bad at waiting. We want results now, but the best things in life take time. Think about planting a tree. If you plant a seed today, you will not wake up to a full-grown tree tomorrow. It takes years of care – water, sunlight, patience. But in the end, you get something strong and lasting, a tree that provides shade, fruit, and fresh air. This idea was tested in one of the most famous psychological studies of all time: the marshmallow experiment. In the late 1960s, psychologist Walter Mischel conducted a study at Stanford University to understand self-control and delayed gratification. Here is how it worked:

Children, usually 4 to 6 years old, were brought into a room one by one. On the table in front of them was a plate with a marshmallow. They were given a choice: eat the marshmallow now, or wait for about 20 minutes and get two more as a reward.

It was a simple test, but it revealed something powerful about human behaviour.

After explaining the rules, the researchers left the children alone with the marshmallow. This was the real test—would they resist the temptation or give in? Some kids could not hold back and ate the marshmallow almost immediately. Others tried creative ways to distract themselves—covering their eyes, turning away, humming songs, even playing games with their hands to avoid thinking about the treat. In the end, about one-third of the children managed to wait the full 20 minutes and earned the extra marshmallows. The rest gave in before time was up.

But the most fascinating part of the study came years later. The researchers followed up with these kids as they grew older and found a striking pattern: the children who had waited tended to perform better in life. They scored higher on tests, did better in school, had more successful careers, and even developed better social skills and healthier habits.

The marshmallow experiment reveals something crucial— self-control and delayed gratification are key predictors of long-term success. Choosing patience over immediate rewards often leads to better outcomes. This lesson applies directly to trading. Traders who focus on the bigger picture— sticking to their strategy instead of chasing quick wins—tend to perform better in the long run.

So, the next time you feel tempted to abandon your trading system for a short-term gain, think about the marshmallow experiment. Success in trading, just like in life, comes to those who wait.

4. Lack of faith in your trading system

Trading a system successfully means having complete faith in its ability to deliver long-term profits. Yet, many traders abandon their systems because they simply do not believe in them fully. There are several deep-rooted reasons for this lack of trust. One major reason is not spending enough time observing the system in action. Many traders jump into a system without giving it enough screen time to see how it performs in different market conditions. Without that experience, it is hard to truly trust that the system will work over time. Just as a gardener needs to see the changing seasons to believe in the cycle of growth, a trader needs to witness the market's ups and downs to have confidence in their system.

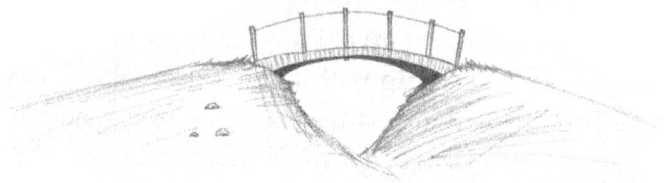

Faith in your system is the bridge that carries you over uncertainty. Without it, every dip looks like a dead end.

Another reason is trading on borrowed conviction. When you use a system based on someone else's ideas without truly understanding it, you lack a personal connection. This "borrowed conviction" quickly falls apart during a losing streak or when unexpected market shifts occur, because it is not rooted in your own experience.

Not doing thorough backtesting can also shake your faith. If you have not tested your system against past data, you will not know how it handles different scenarios. That uncertainty can destroy your confidence when the system hits a rough patch. Here, faith is not just about a blind belief in the system—it is about having absolute faith that holds steady through ups and downs. This is the anchor that keeps you grounded during tough times. Without it, even the best system can be abandoned at the first sign of trouble.

For many traders, this lack of faith creates a cycle of doubt and quitting. They start with enthusiasm, but when losses occur, their confidence wavers. They begin questioning the system, making unnecessary tweaks, or give up altogether. This inconsistency stops them from reaping the long-term benefits of their strategy. Breaking this cycle means building a deep, personal faith in your system—something that only comes with time, experience, and true understanding.

5. Over optimisation

If you ask some of the best traders for their top advice, they would likely say, "Keep your system as simple as possible." A simple system is easy to execute, with fewer steps before making a trading decision. The more variables you add, the harder it becomes to trade in real time. An overly complex system often ends up being just curve-fitted—meaning it worked well in the past because it was tailored to historical data, but that does not guarantee future success. Many traders fall into the trap of over-optimising, believing that complexity equals profitability. This mindset often comes from not fully understanding how markets work. In reality, making money in trading is not about intelligence or having the most sophisticated strategy—it is about execution, discipline, and understanding the game.

Most traders struggle not because the market is too complex, but because they trade without truly understanding market mechanics, build systems based on faulty assumptions, and lack the discipline to follow through. That is what leads to failure, not a lack of complexity in their strategy. A simple test to see if your system is over-complicated is to check your backtested results. If they look overwhelmingly positive in the short term, you have either found the holy grail (unlikely) or over-optimised your strategy to fit past data.

Now that we have covered why traders struggle to stick to a system, let us focus on what can help you overcome these issues and improve as a trader.

HOW TO IMPROVE AS A TRADER

1. The positive feedback loop

This is what the process of an unprofitable trader looks like:

What Most Traders Do

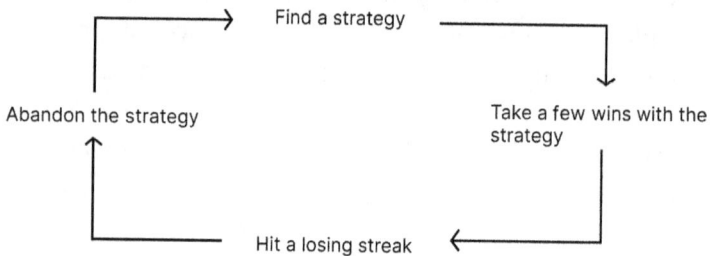

Find a strategy

Abandon the strategy

Take a few wins with the strategy

Hit a losing streak

An unprofitable trader has a tendency to abandon their system completely when they hit a losing streak. In many cases, the fault is not even with the system but with the trader themselves. In my view, abandoning your system completely might not make any sense. The easiest part of trading is finding a good trading strategy. Anyone can do it; stock picking or idea generation is not the difficult part. What is difficult is sticking to a trading system. This is something that only a few traders understand.

On the contrary, here is what the process of a profitable trader looks like. This illustration is enough to help you understand why only a few traders are able to generate consistent money out of the market.

What Profitable Traders Do

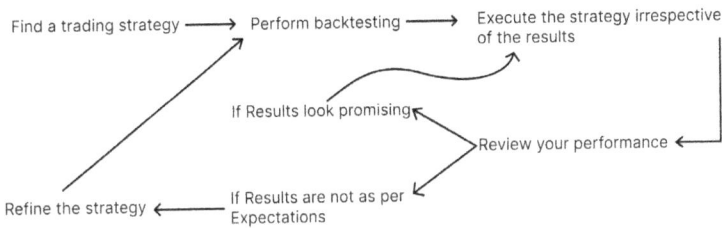

Find a trading strategy ⟶ Perform backtesting ⟶ Execute the strategy irrespective of the results

If Results look promising

Review your performance ←

Refine the strategy ← If Results are not as per Expectations

There are many subtle but crucial steps in a trader's journey that gradually push them toward profitability. A profitable trader begins by choosing a strategy that aligns with their psyche. This is the foundation of a system they can stick with long-term.

Next comes backtesting — a step that cannot be overstated in importance. Backtesting builds conviction, and conviction is what keeps traders from abandoning their system at the first sign of trouble. Without it, the temptation to switch to something new — only to end up back in the cycle of inconsistency — becomes too strong.

Once the system has been tested, the trader moves to live markets. At this stage, the goal is not to obsess over short-term profit and loss but to gather statistically significant data for refinement. This is where unprofitable traders often go wrong — they react emotionally to early results, lose faith, and quit too soon.

After collecting enough live data, the next step is reviewing performance. If the results are good, the trader can continue executing and possibly increase risk if they started conservatively. If the results fall short, the key is to analyse them objectively. Look at the overall data, not just a few trades. Many traders make the mistake of curve-fitting their strategy to a particular period, which can lead to poor real-world performance.

Refining the strategy should always be backed by data, not emotions. Once changes are made, backtesting must be repeated. Even if it means pausing live trading, this step is non-negotiable. Manual backtesting is time-consuming, but skipping it can lead to unnecessary losses. The purpose of revalidation is to ensure that adjustments actually improve the system's performance and that it remains effective across different market conditions. This process strengthens confidence before risking real capital. Patience and thoroughness in these steps can save traders from major setbacks down the road.

2. Developing a long-term mindset

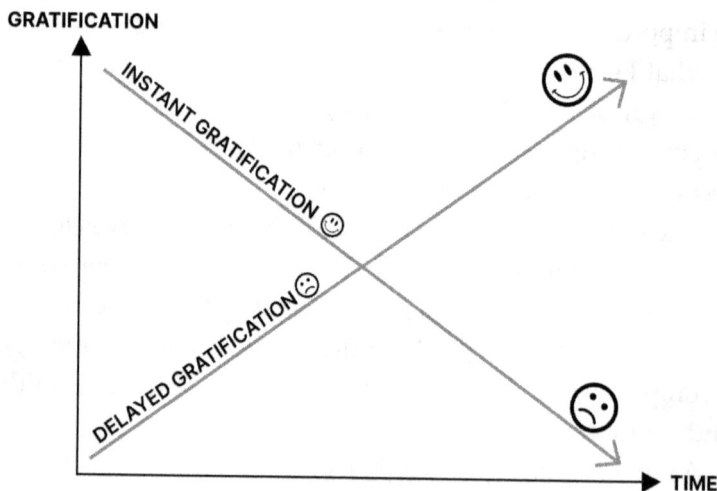

We talked about the marshmallow experiment earlier and concluded that those who have patience and a long-term focus tend to perform better in any area of life. But does this mean you are either born with this ability or not? Are some people just naturally wired for patience while others are not? That is where a follow-up experiment comes in. Researchers divided children into two groups.

The first group was given a set of crayons and promised an even better set later—but the researchers never delivered. Then, they were given stickers with the same promise of more to come, and again, nothing arrived.

The second group received the same promises, but in their case, the researchers followed through.

Later, when both groups participated in the marshmallow experiment, an interesting pattern emerged. The first group—who had learned that promises were not reliable—was far more likely to eat the marshmallow right away. The second group—who had positive experiences with delayed rewards—was more willing to wait for the bigger payoff.

The takeaway? Our past experiences shape our beliefs about delayed gratification. If life has taught you that waiting does not lead to better rewards, you will lean toward instant gratification. But if you have experienced that patience pays off, you are more likely to practise it. This is great news because it means patience is not just something you are born with—it is something you can develop. How? By taking actions that reinforce two key beliefs:

1. Delayed gratification leads to better outcomes.
2. You have the ability to control impulsive urges.

For traders, this applies in a big way. Many struggle to stick to their system because they have not backtested it. They do not fully understand what to expect, so when they hit a drawdown—even a normal one—they panic and abandon the system. But when you have studied historical data and seen how the system performs over time, you are much more likely to trust it and stay the course.

Outside trading, you can build discipline by following through on commitments. Exercise regularly, stick to a diet, complete tasks on time—each time you do what you said you would do, you reinforce the belief that you can trust yourself. The more you build that trust, the easier it becomes to resist short-term impulses, even when they feel tempting in the moment.

3. KISS (Keep It Simple, Stupid)

Imagine you are building the perfect machine. You keep adding parts, thinking each one will improve performance. But at some point, it becomes too complex—so difficult to operate that it barely functions. This is exactly what happens with over-optimised trading systems. On paper, they seem flawless because they have been fine-tuned to fit historical data. But in live markets, they often fail because they are too rigid and cannot adapt to new conditions. Many traders fall into this trap because they want to eliminate all possible losses. They tweak their systems to match every past market movement, hoping to replicate those same profits in the future. But markets do not work that way. The more complicated a system, the harder it is to execute. Too many rules lead to decision paralysis—traders become overwhelmed, second-guessing every move instead of acting with confidence. That is why the best traders prefer simple systems. They build their strategies around a few core principles—rules that are easy to follow and execute, even under pressure. It's like cooking with a few high-quality ingredients instead of following a complicated recipe with dozens of steps. The result is often better and more consistent.

A simple system also reduces the risk of curve-fitting. When you have fewer variables, you are less likely to create a system that only works under specific past conditions. Instead, you develop something robust—an approach that can handle different market environments with ease.

CHAPTER SUMMARY

STICK TO YOUR SYSTEM

SYSTEM HOPPING IS HARMFUL
(HELP) DON'T ABANDON SYSTEMS TRADERS FAIL — ALLOW PROBABILITIES TO PLAY OUT

FIT AND DRAWDOWNS MATTER
ALIGN TRADING SYSTEM WITH PERSONALITY DRAWDOWNS — NORMAL COST OF BUSINESS

LONG TERM FOCUS
AVOID SHORT TERM THINKING SUCCESS REQUIRES PATIENCE DELAYED GRATIFICATION

BUILD FAITH THROUGH KNOWLEDGE
DON'T BORROW CONVICTION DO ADEQUATE BACK TESTING READ AND LEARN

KEEP IT SIMPLE
AVOID OVER OPTIMISATION SIMPLE SYSTEM = EASY EXECUTION

SYSTEM COMPLEXITY ≠ PROFITABILITY

LONG TERM

SIMPLE

FAITH IN KNOWLEDGE

SECTION IV

THE UNENDING GAME: CHALLENGES BEYOND PROFITABILITY

"With great power comes great responsibility."
— Voltaire

Reaching profitability is a significant milestone, but it is not the end of the journey. In this final section, we will address the challenges that persist even after you start making money in the markets. Whether it is dealing with the pressure of expectations—from yourself or others—or managing difficult times when the markets don't go your way, this section will provide strategies to help you stay resilient and maintain your success.

We will also explore how a balanced life outside trading can positively impact your performance, emphasising that good trading is deeply connected to a good life.

CHAPTER 13

HOW TO DEAL WITH DIFFICULT TIMES IN TRADING

"Strength does not come from winning. Your struggles develop your strengths. When you go through hardships and decide not to surrender, that is strength."
— Arnold Schwarzenegger

At some point in your trading journey—whether you are a beginner or have years of experience—you will hit a phase where nothing seems to go your way. Trades that once worked stop working. Strategies that made sense start feeling useless. It is like moving one step forward, only to slide two steps back. During such times, doubt creeps in. You start questioning every decision, sometimes even wondering if you should be trading at all. These crossroads define a trader's future. Some let frustration take over, making emotional mistakes that are hard to recover from. Others stay composed, trusting their process even when things do not go well. Traders who hold their ground are the ones who go on to succeed. But what sets them apart? It is not talent, luck, or some secret strategy. It is a set of simple yet powerful principles that help them push through difficult periods without losing confidence. In this chapter, we will break down those principles—what they are, how they work, and how you can apply them in your own trading. The goal is to give you clarity and reinforce your belief in your system, so you can navigate tough times without getting derailed.

Here are a few key principles to guide you through challenging times:

1. The daily reminder

THE DAILY RESET

DISCIPLINE

FOCUS — CLARITY

RESILIENCE

Over the years, I have been a trader and have also explored different businesses. In this journey, I have met thousands of people from all kinds of backgrounds. I have noticed that people—myself included—tend to forget things that are good for us. Not literally, but in the sense that we take simple, powerful ideas for granted, especially in trading. These are not secrets or rare insights. Most of the time, they are basic truths we already know. Take gratitude, for example. Everyone knows that being grateful is important. But when life gets tough, how often do we remind ourselves of it? If you stop for a moment and appreciate what you have, your perspective changes. Maybe you are struggling right now, but someone else might look at your life and think you have everything they wish for. Gratitude will not magically solve your problems, but it does give you the mental strength to deal with them better. Trading is full of such simple yet powerful ideas. But because we do not remind ourselves of them, we forget. That is why I created something I call my daily reset—a document of key principles I read every single day at a fixed time. I call it a reset because that is exactly what it does. Whether I have had a great winning streak or a rough patch, this daily reminder brings me back to a balanced mindset. It helps me stay focused, calm, and ready to take on the market with the right approach. This habit has made a huge impact on my life. It is hard to explain in words because it is something you have to experience for yourself. But when you make this a daily practice, you will notice a change. Your mindset becomes stronger, your decisions become clearer, and your approach to trading—and life—feels more stable.

This daily reset acts like an anchor. It keeps you connected to what truly matters, so you do not get carried away by the highs of a big win or the frustration of a loss. Trading can be emotionally exhausting, but by revisiting your core principles every day, you stay centred. It also helps you cut out distractions. Markets are full of noise—news, opinions, emotions. If you are not careful, it is easy to get lost in it all. But when you start each day with clear reminders, you filter out what is unnecessary and focus on what actually helps you grow.

Most importantly, this habit builds discipline. It is not about following strict rules but about shaping your mindset in a way that makes you adaptable and resilient. In the long run, that is what makes a trader successful—not some perfect strategy, but the ability to stay composed and make the right decisions under pressure.

So if you are serious about improving—not just as a trader, but in life—consider making your own daily reset. Fill it with lessons that have shaped you, principles that matter to you, and reminders that keep you grounded. And most importantly, commit to reading it every day.

It might seem like a small thing, but over time, this habit can completely transform the way you handle challenges. It will not just help you survive tough times—it will help you thrive, with the confidence and clarity that come from always reminding yourself of what truly matters.

2. The Premortem

Identify Possible Challenges

$\downarrow$

Anticipate Possible Failures

$\downarrow$

Develop Contingency Plans

$\downarrow$

Increased Confidence In Decision Making

Have you ever wished you could make trading decisions with the benefit of hindsight? Imagine how much easier it would be if we could see the present with the same clarity that we see the past. Unfortunately, life does not work that way — we can only understand it backward, but we have to live it forward.

However, there is a way to bridge that gap. The thing we fear most in trading — and in life — is finding ourselves in difficult situations. But the key to overcoming that fear lies in preparation. If you are ready for those tough scenarios in advance, you can create strategies and figure out workarounds before they even happen. This idea comes from a concept called a 'pre-mortem,' which has been around for centuries. Psychologist Gary Klein made it popular, but similar ideas have existed since ancient times. Philosophers and military leaders have long used this kind of thinking to predict problems and prepare for worst-case situations.

The word 'pre-mortem' is based on 'post-mortem,' which is an analysis done after something has already gone wrong. A post-mortem helps people understand what failed and why. Klein's idea was simple: instead of waiting for a failure to happen and then analysing it, why not predict possible failures in advance? That way, you can fix problems before they even occur. This concept is similar to an old Stoic philosophy practice called "premeditatio malorum," which means 'thinking about bad things before they happen.' Stoic philosophers like Seneca and Marcus Aurelius used this to mentally prepare for difficulties in life. They believed that imagining worst-case scenarios would make people stronger and more prepared when problems actually occurred. The modern pre-mortem works the same way — it helps you see risks ahead of time so you can deal with them better.

As a trader, your success depends on being ready for anything. The more prepared you are, the better your decisions will be. But if something unexpected happens and you are not ready, you will likely panic and make impulsive choices — and impulsive choices rarely lead to consistent success. So, your goal as a trader is to think ahead about everything that could go wrong.

What if your broker's platform crashes?
What if a stock suddenly moves against you?
What if the power goes out right when the market opens?
What if your internet stops working?

Now, you might think, "Is this not just making me paranoid?" Actually, it is the opposite. This is not about making you anxious — it is about making you confident. When you are prepared for the worst, you will not panic. You will stay calm while others are scrambling. And that is what will set you apart in the long run. Most traders get shaken up by unexpected problems. But you will be ready. You will make better decisions because you have already thought through the risks. That is what separates winning traders from the rest — it is not that they avoid problems, but that they know exactly how to handle them when they come.

3. Zoom out

If you have been feeling stuck lately — like nothing is working, and every effort seems to go nowhere — it might be time to take a step back and zoom out. When you zoom out and look at your trading journey from a bigger perspective, what do you see? If your progress looks like a slow, upward climb with some dips along the way, then you do not need to worry.

Frustration often comes from comparing ourselves to others. But the truth is that comparing yourself to others is not helpful. Everyone has different backgrounds, risk tolerance, and personal situations, so it does not make sense to measure your success using someone else's standards. Your real competition is yourself. If you are better today than you were six months ago, you are on the right track. Progress is not a straight line — it moves in waves, with ups and downs. What matters is that the overall direction is up.

Now, let us take this idea of zooming out even further. Imagine your trading journey as a map. If you zoom in too much, all you see are the sharp turns, roadblocks, and dead ends. It feels overwhelming. But when you zoom out, the full path becomes clear. You realise that the twists and turns are not the whole story — they are just part of the journey. In the middle of a tough phase, it is easy to forget how far you have come. But if you zoom out, you will see things differently.

That struggle you are facing right now? It is just one chapter in a much bigger book. Like any good story, there will be ups and downs. What matters is how the whole story unfolds over time.

Zooming out also helps you focus on what truly matters. It is easy to get caught up in daily market fluctuations, obsessing over every tiny move up or down. But when you zoom out, you realise those short-term moves are just noise. What really matters is the long-term trend and the steady progress you are making over time. Success in trading — and in life — is not about winning big every time. It is about showing up consistently, making smart choices, and letting small wins add up over time.

Zooming out helps you appreciate the journey instead of getting stuck on every setback.

Lastly, zooming out reminds you to be patient. Growth takes time, and sometimes it may seem like you are not making any progress. But when you step back and look at the bigger picture, you will see that every small step brings you closer to your goals.

So the next time you feel like you are going nowhere, take a deep breath and zoom out. Look at how far you have come, focus on your own journey, and trust that as long as you keep moving forward, you are on the right path.

The road may not be straight, but every step is leading you toward your destination.

4. The power of combinatorial decisions

Sometimes, the hardest moments in trading are not just about losses or emotional struggles—they come when you hit a wall trying to solve a problem. You might feel stuck, unable to decide between two possible solutions. It is something every trader, including myself, has faced. I have always been someone who thinks deeply, analysing things from every angle. That is useful in many ways, but it can also be exhausting—especially when you are stuck between two choices and cannot figure out the best one.

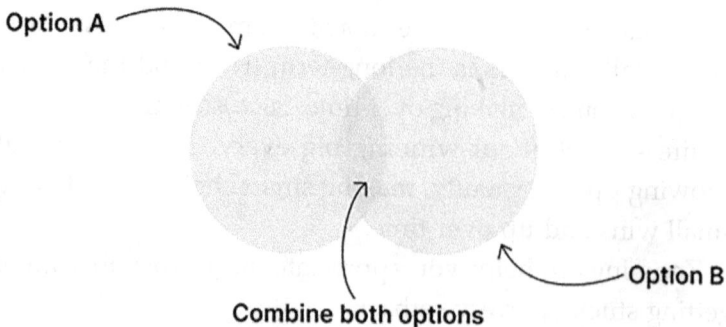

Option A

Option B

Combine both options

Often, the issue is not that there is no solution—it is that there are multiple solutions, each with its own pros and cons, making it tough to pick just one. We are taught that life is about making choices, that we need to pick a path and commit to it. But what if that is not always the best approach? What if the real answer is not choosing between X and Y, but finding a way to use both? This is where combinatorial thinking comes in. Instead of seeing options as separate or conflicting, why not explore how they can work together? By blending different strategies, you can create a stronger solution that takes advantage of the best parts of each while reducing their weaknesses. For example, if you are debating between two trading strategies—one aggressive, one conservative—you do not have to choose just one.

You could create a hybrid approach that combines elements of both. This way, you get the benefits of both strategies while managing the risks. In many cases, combining solutions leads to better clarity and more consistent results. It removes the pressure of making a final, either-or decision and opens up new ways to solve problems. Since I started thinking this way, I have found that it helps not just in trading, but in many areas of life.

So, the next time you are stuck between two choices, ask yourself: Do you really have to pick just one? Sometimes, the best way forward is to take the strongest parts of both options and create something even better.

5. Keep your trading size in sync with the market

One of the biggest mistakes traders make is using the same position size all the time. The common advice is to keep your size consistent because wins and losses are unpredictable. In theory, that makes sense. But in real trading, it is not always the best approach. Markets change, and so does your mindset. Sometimes, the market is full of good opportunities, and you are in the right mental space to take advantage of them. In those moments, trading with a larger size makes sense because you are more confident and likely to perform well. But then there are tough periods—when good setups are rare, you force trades, and your mental game is off.

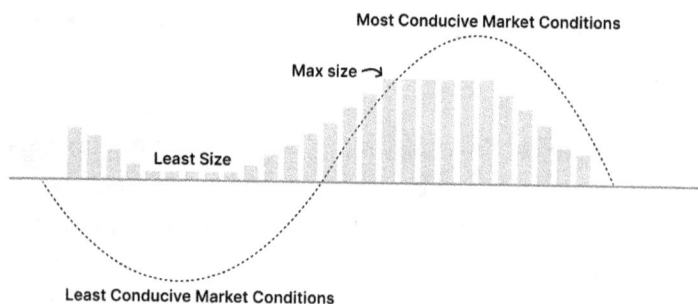

Now, think about it: Does it make sense to use the same position size in a rough patch as you would in a strong one? Of course not. Yet, many traders do exactly that. It is like trying to dig yourself out of a hole by digging deeper. Some of the biggest trading mistakes happen when you push too hard to recover losses. The smarter move would be to reduce your size. When things are not going well, trading smaller helps limit your losses and gives you the space to regain your composure. The goal is not to recover quickly—it is to rebuild your confidence step by step. Lowering your size does not mean you are giving up. It means you are focusing on the process, not just the results. During tough times, the goal is not to hit big wins but to take small, steady trades that keep you moving forward. As conditions improve and you start seeing more high-quality setups, that is when you can slowly increase your size again. Gradually bring it back to normal as your confidence returns and the market aligns in your favour.

How do you know if you are in a bad period? A simple way is to look at your recent trades. If the last few have not worked out well, it might be time to step back and reassess. Focus on your watchlist, review what has been going wrong, and adjust your position size accordingly.

The key to long-term success is adaptability. If you can adjust your size based on both market conditions and your own mindset, you will stay in control—no matter what the market throws at you.

6. Take a short break

Step back, breathe, reset. The market will be there when you return.

Believe it or not, one of the best ways to handle tough times in trading is to take a short break. Sometimes, the problem is not the market or your strategy—it is you. The human mind is unpredictable. Some days, you are in sync with the market, spotting opportunities with ease. On other days, nothing seems to go right. You keep missing trades, and it feels like everyone else is making money except you.

Your mindset plays a huge role in trading. If you are feeling overwhelmed, frustrated, or mentally drained, it will show in your decisions. When you reach this point, it is important to recognise that you are not in the best state to trade effectively. Instead of forcing your way through and risking bigger mistakes, sometimes the best move is to step away. Close your positions, shut down your screen, and allow yourself to do something completely unrelated to trading.

Taking a break does not mean quitting — it means resetting. It gives your mind the space it needs to clear up and regain focus. Whether it is for a few hours, a day, or even a week, stepping back can help you return with fresh energy and a clearer perspective.

Use this time to relax and recharge. Spend time with family, pursue a hobby, exercise, or simply enjoy being outdoors. The goal is to disconnect from the stress of trading and let your mind reset.

When you return, you will likely notice a shift. You will see opportunities more clearly, make better decisions, and trade with more confidence. Taking a break is not a sign of weakness — it is a strategy to make sure you trade at your best.

So, the next time you feel stuck, stressed, or out of sync, remember: it is okay to step away. A short break might be exactly what you need to get back on track, refreshed and ready to go.

CHAPTER SUMMARY

HOW TO DEAL WITH DIFFICULT TIMES in TRADING

DAILY REMINDER
CREATE "DAILY RESET" DOCUMENT
GUIDING PRINCIPLES FOR BALANCED MINDSET
APPROACH TRADING WITH FRESH OUTLOOK

THE PREMORTEM
PREPARE FOR POTENTIAL PROBLEMS
CREATE BACKUP PLANS TO HANDLE UNEXPECTED SITUATIONS

ZOOM OUT
TAKE LONG TERM PERSPECTIVE
FOCUS ON OVERALL PROGRESS THAN SHORT TERM SETBACKS

COMBINATORIAL DECISIONS
EXPLORE COMBINING DIFFERENT STRATEGIES WHEN FACING TOUGH CHOICES

LOWER YOUR TRADING SIZE
REDUCE YOUR POSITION SIZE DURING DIFFICULT PERIODS TO MINIMIZE POTENTIAL LOSSES

PREPARE   COMBINE   PRINCIPLES

14

MASTERING CONSISTENCY

"Success is the result of preparation, hard work,
and learning from failure."
— Colin Powell

Consistency is one of the most important yet misunderstood parts of trading. When traders hear the word 'consistency,' many immediately think of their profit and loss (P&L) or equity curve. They assume that a consistent trader is someone who makes money every single day.

But that is not the kind of consistency that really matters. The real goal is to be consistent in your trading process. This difference is so important because the market is unpredictable. No matter how skilled or experienced you are, there will be days, weeks, or even months when the market does not favour your strategy. If you believe consistency means always winning, you are setting yourself up for frustration and disappointment. Instead, the consistency you should aim for is in how you approach your trades—your discipline, process, and mindset. These are the things you can control. You see, you cannot control the market, but you can control how you respond to it. By following your trading process every day, you give yourself the best chance of long-term success. This means sticking to your plan, managing risk, and not letting short-term ups and downs shake your confidence.

As we move forward, we will explore why consistency in your process matters more than consistency in your results. I will discuss why you do not need to learn from every single trade, the value of sticking to one strategy, and why good trading often feels boring. I will also cover the dangers of false positives—those lucky trades that make you feel invincible—and why stop-losses are actually your best friend.

SECRETS TO KEEPING A BALANCED OUTLOOK

Consistency in your process is what separates professional traders from amateurs. It is what helps you stay in the game, even when things do not go your way. And most importantly, it is what leads to sustainable profitability.

"Desire consistency in your process, not in your outcomes."

1. Do not try to learn from every trade

You have probably heard the advice, "Every loss is an opportunity to learn." It sounds wise, doesn't it? But if you take this idea too literally, you might be in for a surprise. Profitable trading often requires a different mindset—you do not need to learn from every single trade. Let me explain why. When you start trading, the most important thing is to have a well-tested system. This means you have already done the hard work—backtesting, refining, and ensuring

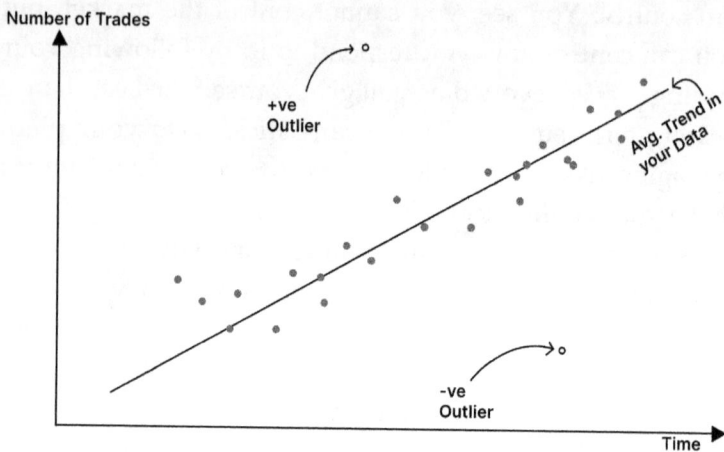

your strategy works over a large sample of trades. Once you go live, the key is to stick to your system for at least 100 trades before making any major adjustments because the outcome of any one trade is often random. You could follow your system perfectly and still take a loss, or you could break your rules and still win.

If you try to extract a lesson from every trade, you might end up chasing patterns that do not actually mean anything. A single loss does not mean your strategy is flawed — it could just be randomness at play. If you start making changes based on individual trades, you risk forming unreliable beliefs — ones based on luck rather than solid data. Instead, focus on recurring patterns that appear over many trades. If you notice consistent issues over a larger sample, then it makes sense to refine your approach.

But tweaking your system after every win or loss? That is just reacting to noise. So, trust your process. Stick to your tested system, and resist the urge to constantly adjust it based on short-term results. This discipline will help you avoid emotional overreactions and keep you on the path to long-term success.

2. The importance of sticking to one thing

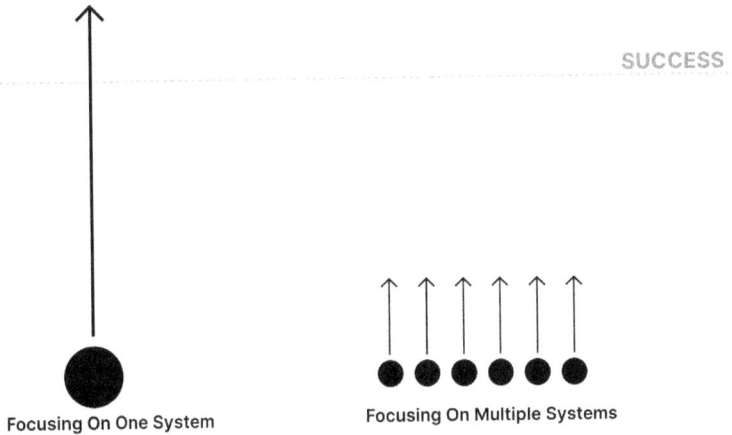

SUCCESS

Focusing On One System   Focusing On Multiple Systems

One of the biggest challenges traders face is sticking to their system. Many people assume that making money in the markets requires a complex, sophisticated strategy. But in reality, some of the most profitable trading systems are surprisingly simple.

The hard part is actually following them consistently. Even the best trading systems go through rough patches where they do not perform as well as you would like. It is during these times that traders start doubting their strategy. The temptation to jump to a different system or tweak your approach can be strong. You might start experimenting with new methods or taking trades you normally would not—just to break out of the slump. But this is where many traders go wrong. When you introduce random changes to your trading, you get random results. It is like throwing darts while blindfolded—sometimes you will hit the target, but more often than not, you will miss. This lack of consistency is what prevents traders from achieving long-term profitability.

The truth is, sticking to one system, even when it is struggling, is crucial for long-term success. It is about having the discipline to trust your strategy and not let short-term results shake your confidence. Trading is simple, but it is not easy. And the ability to stay the course when things get tough is what separates professional traders from those who struggle.

3. Good trading is boring

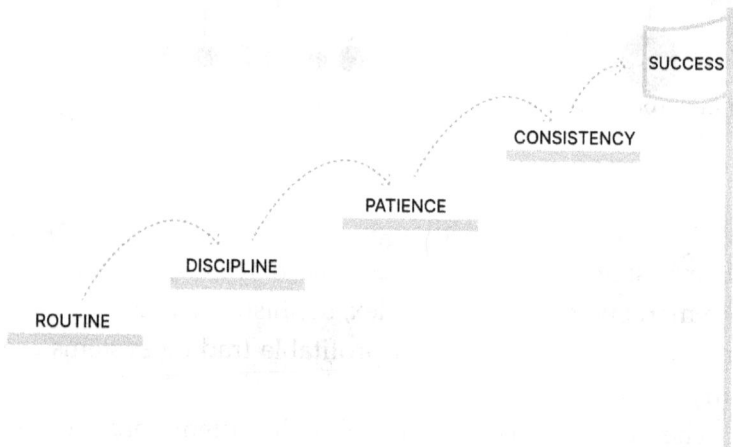

SUCCESS

CONSISTENCY

PATIENCE

DISCIPLINE

ROUTINE

Social media makes trading look like a life of endless excitement, luxury, and adrenaline. One day, a trader is lounging in Dubai. The next, they are on a yacht in Miami, making millions with just a few clicks. It is a glamorous illusion—one that makes trading seem all about fast money, high stakes, and non-stop thrills.

But the reality is that good trading is actually pretty boring. Successful trading is not about making reckless bets or riding emotional highs and lows. It is about following a routine, sticking to your plan, and making logical decisions — every single day. Most of the time, trading means sitting at your screen, analysing charts, waiting patiently for the right setup, and executing trades with precision. There is no room for impulsive decisions. The excitement that social media glorifies is just noise that distracts new traders from what really matters.

For professional traders, the routine can feel monotonous — because they do not chase excitement; they chase consistency. They know that the thrill of big wins can lead to big losses if they are not careful. Instead of seeking the next adrenaline rush, they focus on slow, steady, and reliable trades that align with their long-term vision.

Good trading feels repetitive because it is. You follow the same process, apply the same rules, and control your emotions — day in and day out. That discipline is what leads to success, not the flashy lifestyle you see online. In fact, the more boring your trading becomes, the better you are probably doing. It means you are sticking to your system and not getting distracted by market hype. It is easy to get caught up in the social media fantasy of trading, but real success does not come from chasing thrills. It comes from mastering patience, discipline, and consistency — even when it feels mundane.

4. Stop-losses are not bad

Losses are tough for many traders. It is easy to believe that a good trader never loses or that losses mean failure. But that could not be further from the truth. Losses are not just inevitable in trading — they are necessary. Understanding this is key to long-term success. Think of losses as the cost of doing business. Just like a shop owner needs to buy inventory before making sales, a trader needs to take losses to uncover profitable trades.

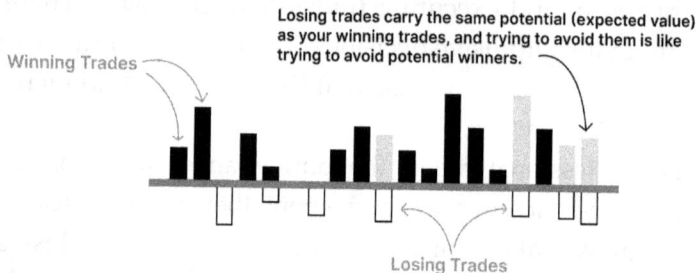

Losing trades carry the same potential (expected value) as your winning trades, and trying to avoid them is like trying to avoid potential winners.

Winning Trades

Losing Trades

The idea is simple: every trade has a probability of success and failure. No matter how good your system is, not every trade will be a winner. Losses are just the other side of the coin. They balance out your wins and make the system work.

If you never take a loss, it could mean you are not trading enough—or just riding a lucky streak. But luck is not a strategy. In the long run, what matters is consistently following your system. And that system includes taking losses.

When you take a loss according to your plan, it is not a failure—it is simply part of executing your edge. Your system is designed to win over a series of trades, not on every single one. That is why losses should not be feared or avoided. They are part of the process.

The real problem starts when traders try to outsmart their own system just to avoid losses. They let fear or frustration take over and make decisions outside their plan. But in doing so, they abandon the very thing that gives them an edge: their system. Trying to avoid losses by breaking your rules does not just stop you from losing—it stops you from winning too. From a mathematical perspective, every trading system has an expected value—a measure of its long-term profitability. This expected value is shaped by both wins and losses. While the wins bring in profits, the losses are what keep the system balanced. Without them, the edge disappears. Think of it like trying to balance a scale by adding weight to only one side—it just does not work.

So, the next time you take a loss, do not see it as a failure. Instead, recognise it for what it is: a necessary step toward long-term profitability. You are not trying to avoid losses at all costs—you are following a system that, over time, will generate more wins than losses.That is where true consistency and success in trading lie.

5. Develop probabilistic thinking

Probabilistic thinking might sound complicated at first, but once you get it, it completely changes how you approach trading. It is about understanding that trading is not about certainty—you can never know exactly what will happen next. Instead, it is about working with probabilities—the chances of different outcomes—and making decisions based on them over a large number of trades.

Think of it like rolling dice. Each trade is just one roll in a long series. Whether this particular trade wins or loses is not the focus. What matters is whether your overall approach makes money over time. This shift in thinking is crucial because it takes away the pressure of being right every single time. And that is important because trying to be right all the time can really mess with your head as a trader.

WHY IS PROBABILISTIC THINKING
ESSENTIAL IN TRADING?

Trading is a numbers game, not a guessing game. Once you start thinking in probabilities, you realise that each trade — whether it is a win or a loss — is just a small part of a bigger picture. This is where expected value comes in, a concept we touched on earlier. Expected value is simply the average profit you can expect from each trade if you follow the same strategy over and over again. For example, let us say your trading system wins 60% of the time. If each winning trade gives you 2% profit and each losing trade costs you 1%, then your expected value per trade is 0.8%.

Expected Value = (Probability of Winning * Winning %) - (Probability of Losing * Losing %)

Expected Value = (0.60 * 2) - (0.40 * 1)

Expected Value = (1.2) - (0.4)

Expected Value = 0.8%

With Similar Stats you can expect to generate about 0.8% return on each trade on average over a large enough sample size.

This might not seem like a big deal, but when you apply it over hundreds or thousands of trades, the impact is huge. It means that, on average, you are making money with every trade you take — even if some trades end up as losses. This matters because it helps you stay focused and stick to your system, even when things are not going well in the short term. Instead of panicking after a few losses and doubting your entire strategy, you remind yourself that losses are just a part of the bigger picture.

As long as you keep following your system with discipline, the probabilities will work in your favour over time.

THE KEY CONCEPTS BEHIND PROBABILISTIC THINKING

To really get probabilistic thinking, you need to grasp a few key concepts:

1. The Law of Large Numbers

This is a basic rule in probability theory which applies perfectly to trading. It simply means that the more you repeat something (like placing trades), the closer you get to the expected results. In trading, this means your system's true edge only shows up over a large number of trades — not just a few. That is why it is so important not to judge your system — or yourself — based on a handful of wins or losses.

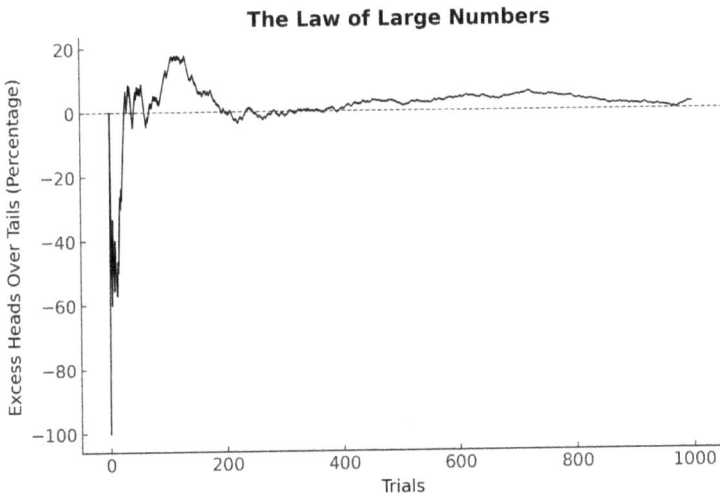

The Law of Large Numbers

2. Expected value

As discussed earlier, expected value helps you calculate the average profit per trade by factoring in both wins and losses. Once you understand this, you start seeing every trade—win or loss—as a step toward long-term success. It is like earning an invisible profit each time you stick to your rules, no matter what happens with that one trade.

3. Risk management

Probabilistic thinking and risk management always go together. Since you cannot predict the result of any single trade, the only way to stay in the game is by managing your risk properly. This means making sure that no single loss can cause major damage to your account. You do this by setting stop-losses, controlling your position size, and accepting that losses are just a normal part of trading.

A lot of traders struggle with this because they want to avoid losses at all costs. But the truth is, losses are not the problem—big, uncontrolled losses are. When you keep each loss small and follow your system, you allow the probabilities to work in your favour over time. This is how professional traders survive the ups and downs of the market while still coming out ahead in the long run.

INTEGRATING PROBABILISTIC THINKING INTO YOUR TRADING

So, how do you start thinking probabilistically in your trading? It starts with a mindset shift. You need to move away from the idea that every trade needs to be a winner and embrace the reality that losses are just part of the journey.

Here are a few practical steps to help you integrate probabilistic thinking:

1. Focus on the process, not the outcome

Instead of obsessing over whether a trade was a winner or a loser, ask yourself whether you followed your system's rules. If you did, then you are on the right track, regardless of the immediate result. Over time, this approach will help you build confidence in your system and reduce the emotional rollercoaster that comes with trading.

2. Embrace the long game

Understand that trading is a marathon, not a sprint. The goal is not to win every trade but to make consistent, small gains that add up over time. By thinking probabilistically, you play the long game, where the edge of your system can truly shine.

3. Detach yourself from the outcome of individual trades

Probabilistic thinking helps you detach emotionally from the outcome of any single trade. You start to see each trade as just one in a long series, where the goal is to execute your edge consistently. This detachment is crucial because it allows you to make rational decisions, even in the face of losses.

When you really accept probabilistic thinking, you stop seeing trading as a series of isolated events and start seeing it as a continuous process. You understand that every trade, win or lose, is part of a larger picture. As long as follow your system's rules, you are moving closer to your long-term goals.

Just remember this: consistency in trading is not about winning every trade. It is about consistently executing your process with discipline and patience, knowing that over time, the probabilities will work in your favour.

By focusing on the process and embracing probabilistic thinking, you are setting yourself up for long-term success in the trading world.

CHAPTER SUMMARY
CONSISTENCY
CONSISTENCY IN PROCESS NOT OUTCOME
APPLY CONSISTENTLY TRADING STRATEGY RISK MANAGEMENT MINDSET THAN FIXATING ON DAILY PROFITS
STICK TO YOUR SYSTEM
AVOID CONSTANT TWEAKING OF STRATEGY TRUST AND ADHERE TO WELL-TESTED SYSTEM
GOOD TRADING IS BORING
DISCIPLINE, ROUTINE LOGICAL DECISIONS V/S EXCITEMENT AND ADRENALIN
embrace YOUR LOSSES
LOSS
ACCEPT LOSS AS PART OF DOING BUSINESS LOSSES ARE INEVITABLE & NECESSARY
THINK PROBABILISTICALLY
PROFIT
FOCUS ON OVERALL PROBABILITY OF SUCCESS
CONSISTENCY
SYSTEM
EMBRACE

15

HANDLING THE PRESSURE OF EXPECTATIONS

"Expectations are premeditated resentments."
— Anne Lamott

Livermore made and lost several fortunes throughout his career, but what often gets overlooked is the immense pressure he faced—not just from the market but from the people around him. His success brought admiration, but it also created expectations that he would always win, always be ahead of the game. This kind of pressure can be suffocating, even for the best traders.

When you start trading, you might not feel this kind of weight immediately. But as you grow, as people see you making money, the expectations will start creeping in. Family, friends, maybe even random acquaintances—will all have their own ideas about what you should be doing, how much you should be making, and how you should be living. Whether you realise it or not, these external voices can start influencing your decisions. The real danger here is when expectations start controlling your actions. You might take unnecessary risks just to prove yourself. You might avoid cutting a loss because admitting a mistake feels like failure. You might overtrade just to meet some imaginary standard. But trading does not work that way. The market does not care about expectations — it only responds to discipline, risk management, and probability. The solution is not to ignore expectations entirely. Instead, it is about knowing which ones to keep and which ones to let go of. Set goals that are based on your own process, not on impressing others. Understand that losses do not mean failure, they are just part of the game. And most importantly, remind yourself that the only expectations that truly matter are the ones that help you stay consistent and grow as a trader.

THE RISE OF JESSE LIVERMORE

Jesse Livermore was a legendary figure in the world of trading, often referred to as the 'Boy Plunger' for his ability to short the market and make enormous profits. He began his trading career as a young man, starting out in bucket shops and quickly making a name for himself with his bold and highly successful trades. By the time he was in his twenties, Livermore had amassed a fortune, and his reputation as a brilliant trader was firmly established.

The Weight of Expectations

Livermore's growing success brought not just wealth but also intense pressure — both from within and from those around him. People saw him as a market genius, someone who could predict price movements with incredible accuracy.

This reputation created a heavy expectation for him to keep winning, no matter what. He himself set sky-high standards, demanding perfection in his trades. He was not satisfied with just making money—he wanted to prove, again and again, that he was the best. This mindset pushed him to take bigger risks, always chasing the next big profit. But it was not just his own expectations that weighed on him. As a public figure, he was always in the spotlight. The financial world followed his every move, and there was silent pressure on him to keep delivering. Every loss felt not just like a financial setback, but also like a blow to his image. Over time, this pressure became overwhelming, making it harder for him to trade with a clear mind.

When everyone expects you to fly, even standing still feels like failure.

The psychological toll

The weight of these expectations had a deep effect on Livermore's mind. His success had given him wealth and fame, but it had also left him feeling isolated. He was no longer just trading for himself — he was trading for the people who believed in him, for his investors, and for the reputation he had built over the years. This constant pressure slowly ate away at his confidence, filling his mind with doubt and anxiety.

When the market turned against him, the stress only grew worse. He was not just dealing with financial losses—he was battling the fear of failing in front of the world. The burden of living up to his image clouded his judgment, and instead of following the careful strategies that had once made him successful, he started making impulsive decisions driven by emotion. This shift in mindset led to heavy losses, and the mental strain started affecting not just his trading but also his personal life. The very thing that had made him great—his ability to stay disciplined and calculated—was now slipping away under the weight of expectations.

The downward spiral

Livermore's struggle with expectations led to a series of financial collapses. Despite his earlier victories, he went bankrupt multiple times. And with each downfall, the pressure to recover and prove himself only grew heavier. Every failure deepened the burden he carried, making it harder for him to regain his confidence.

In the end, the pressure became unbearable. The losses, the personal struggles, and the constant need to live up to his reputation took a devastating toll on him. In 1940, Livermore took his own life, leaving behind a note that reflected his overwhelming sense of failure.

His story is a reminder of how even the most brilliant traders can break under the weight of expectations when they become too much to handle.

LESSONS LEARNED

Jesse Livermore's story is a strong reminder of how expectations — both from within and from others — can affect even the best traders.

His life shows how the pressure to maintain a certain image or standard can lead to poor decisions, emotional stress, and, in extreme cases, personal downfall.

While his case was extreme, the underlying problem is something many traders face. The pressure to succeed can create a mental state where logic takes a backseat to fear and anxiety. The need to prove oneself can lead to impulsive decisions, making trading much harder than it needs to be.

Moving ahead, we will break down expectations — where they come from, how they influence our trading, and most importantly, how to handle them in a way that keeps us on the right path. Expectations will always be there.

The key is not to escape them but to learn how to manage them without letting them control us.

1. Recognising the source of expectations

The first step in handling expectations is understanding where they come from. Some expectations come from within — from our own goals, ambitions, and desires. These can be the hardest to manage because they are closely tied to our self-worth. We push ourselves because we want to succeed, prove something, or feel a sense of achievement.

Then there are expectations from others—family, friends, colleagues, and even society. Some are direct, like when a family member hopes you will achieve financial security. Others are unspoken, like the quiet pressure to maintain a certain lifestyle or reputation.

In Jesse Livermore's case, he faced both. He had high expectations of himself, always aiming for bigger successes, but he also felt the eyes of the financial world watching him. This combination made things even harder, as he was not just trading for himself—he was trading to meet expectations that kept growing with every win.

2. The psychological impact of expectations

Expectations, especially when they are unrealistic or excessive, can have a profound psychological impact. They can create a constant state of stress and anxiety, as you are always trying to meet or exceed the bar that has been set.

This stress can lead to a number of issues, including:

- **Decision-making paralysis**
  When you are under too much pressure to succeed, every decision starts feeling like a life-or-death situation. This can make you overthink so much that you end up stuck, unable to decide anything at all. In trading, this could mean missing good opportunities or freezing at important moments.
- **Overtrading**
  At the same time, the pressure to meet expectations can push you into overtrading. You might feel like you have to keep proving yourself, which can lead

to impulsive trades driven by emotions rather than a solid strategy. This was a major issue for Livermore, especially when he was trying to recover from losses and maintain his reputation.

- **Emotional exhaustion**
  Always pushing to meet high expectations can take a toll on your mental and emotional well-being. The fear of failure, the stress of not meeting the mark, and the pressure to always be at your best can drain you. When you are emotionally exhausted, staying focused, making clear decisions, and sticking to your trading plan becomes much harder.

3. Strategies for managing expectations

Managing expectations does not mean lowering your standards or giving up on your goals. It simply means finding a balance where you can chase your dreams without feeling overwhelmed by the pressure.

Here are some strategies to help you manage expectations more effectively:

1. Setting the right goals

One of the best things you can do is set goals that are realistic and achievable. It is good to aim high, but your goals should also match reality. This means knowing your current skills, understanding market conditions, and setting a reasonable time frame. If your goals are too big and unrealistic, you might end up feeling disappointed and under too much pressure.

2. Practise self-compassion

Be kind to yourself. Setbacks are a normal part of trading, and they do not define your skills or worth. Self-compassion means recognising your efforts and progress, even when things do not go your way. This helps you feel less pressure to be perfect and lets you learn from mistakes without being too hard on yourself.

3. Communicate with loved ones

If you feel pressured by others' expectations, talking to the people around you can help. Share what you are going through and the challenges you are facing. Many times, we assume others expect more from us than they actually do. Being open about it can reduce some of this pressure and help you get the support you need.

4. Focus on the process, not just the outcome

Instead of stressing over specific results, focus on the trading process itself. This means paying attention to how you improve your skills, learn from experiences, and make better decisions.

When you shift your focus to the process, you will feel less pressureed to achieve certain outcomes and start appreciating the progress you make along the way.

5. Limit external influences

Today, it is easy to feel pressured by social media, peers, or industry standards. To avoid this, focus on your own journey instead of getting distracted by others. Every individual's path is different, and constantly comparing yourself can create unnecessary stress. Every trader faces the pressure of expectations at some point. Whether it comes from within or from others, learning to manage this pressure is key to staying mentally strong and succeeding in trading.

Jesse Livermore's story is a strong reminder of why managing expectations matters. His success and failures were not just about market conditions or trading strategies — they were deeply linked to the weight of expectations. Understanding where your own expectations come from, recognising their psychological impact, and using the right strategies to handle them can help you stay clear-headed and resilient in your trading journey.

At its core, trading is as much a mental challenge as it is a technical one. By strengthening your mindset, being kind to yourself, and focusing on the process rather than just the results, you can find a healthy balance — one that lets you chase your goals without being crushed by the pressure.

CHAPTER SUMMARY

HANDLING THE PRESSURE OF EXPECTATIONS

EXPECTATIONS ARE DOUBLE-EDGED SWORD — THEY MOTIVATE BUT ALSO CREATE PRESSURE CAN LEAD TO SELF DOUBT

UNDERSTAND THE SOURCE — SELF IMPOSED (TIED TO IDENTITY) OR EXTERNAL (FROM FAMILY/SOCIETY)

PSYCHOLOGICAL IMPACT — STRESS, OVERTRADING DECISION MAKING PARALYSIS OVERTRADING EMOTIONAL EXHAUSTION

MANAGE EFFECTIVELY — SET REALISTIC GOALS PRACTICE SELF-COMPASSION COMMUNICATE WITH LOVED 1s FOCUS ON TRADING PROCESS

LEARN FROM JESSE LIVERMORE — IMPORTANCE OF MANAGING EXPECTATIONS TO AVOID PSYCHOLOGICAL STRAIN MAKE SOUND DECISIONS

MANAGE

UNDERSTAND

SELF COMPASSION

16

THE TOUGH CHALLENGE OF SCALING UP

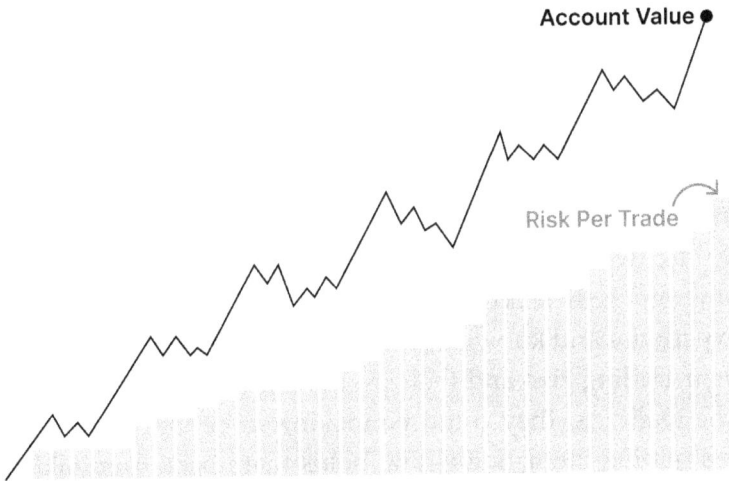

Account Value

Risk Per Trade

Scaling up is one of those tricky problems that every serious trader faces at some point. Even after figuring out a profitable strategy, the question of how to increase trade size and grow their account remains a major challenge.

It is not a small hurdle. To many, it feels like an enormous wall—one they keep hitting but cannot seem to climb over. What is surprising, and maybe even frustrating, is how common this problem is. I have seen traders who have been in the markets for five, seven, even ten years still struggling with it. They have put in the effort, mastered their strategy, and found consistency. They make steady profits, staying in the game, but somehow, they get stuck. They cannot seem to break through to the next level—to grow their size and scale up the way they want to. I know this feeling first hand because I have been there myself. It is not just frustrating—it is confusing—like standing in front of a massive wall, trying every possible way to get over it, but nothing works. You push harder, put in more effort, but something keeps holding you back. You know you have the potential, you can see the other side, yet it remains just out of reach.

It gets even more confusing when you look at traders who have been making good money for years—people who were earning $50,000 or even $100,000 a month a few years ago—and they still make the same amount today. At first glance, that does not seem like a problem. Most people would be thrilled with that kind of income. But when you consider how much their account size has grown, along with their experience and knowledge, it starts to seem strange. Should their trading size and their profits not have increased too? The reality is, they could be making more, but something is stopping them. Something holds them back from taking bigger trades, managing larger risks, and pushing their limits.

Why does this happen? Why do so many traders, even after mastering their strategy, struggle to scale up? Why do they stay at the same level year after year, despite everything else about their trading improving? From what I have seen, there are several reasons traders get stuck in this cycle. More importantly, there are solutions. Breaking free from this rut is not easy, but it is possible—if you understand the technical and psychological barriers at play.

In this chapter, we will dig into these reasons. We will uncover what really stops traders from increasing their size, and most crucially, what they can do to fix it. Scaling up is a tough challenge, but with the right mindset and approach, it is absolutely within reach. Let us see how this can be done.

1. Let go of emotional attachment to trade outcomes

Detach from the money. Focus on the process. The game rewards those who stay in it long enough.

One of the biggest roadblocks traders face when they try to scale up is their inability to detach from the outcome of each trade. They do not just see the money they put in as numbers on a screen—they think about what that money could buy, how it could impact their life. In doing so, they amplify the emotions tied to every win and loss. Over time, traders become comfortable trading a small size because that amount feels insignificant to their overall financial situation. But the moment they try to increase their size, the pressure kicks in. Suddenly, every loss feels heavier. They start calculating what they could have bought with the money they just lost, or worse, they spiral into a 'what if' mindset—what if this loss is just the beginning of a bigger drawdown? What if I lose even more?

But the truth is none of this is real—it is all in your head. If you want to scale up successfully, you need to accept one fundamental fact about trading: wins and losses are random. You can never predict with certainty which trade will be a winner or a loser. Even the best trading strategies go through winning and losing streaks, but those streaks mean nothing on their own. Trying to guess which trade will be "the one" is like trying to predict which way the dice will roll—completely pointless. The real game is about long-term consistency, not the outcome of a single trade. Your focus should always be on executing your system with discipline, knowing that, over time, your edge will play out. If you stick to the process, the results will take care of themselves.

A common mistake traders make is thinking of their trading capital as something personal—something to protect at all costs. This is like a carpenter believing that his tools alone determine the quality of his work. But a skilled carpenter knows that the real key to craftsmanship is not the tools, but how they are used. The same goes for trading. Your capital is not what makes you successful—it is how you manage it. Instead of focusing on whether you win or lose today, think of your money as the fuel that allows you to keep participating in the market. Each trade is an opportunity, not a life-or-death event.

Risk, when viewed correctly, is not something to fear but something to embrace. It is the cost of doing business. By risking only a small percentage of your capital on each trade, you do not gamble your future—you put yourself in the best position to take advantage of the right opportunities when they come. One simple shift in mindset can help: stop thinking of your trading capital as real money you could spend on other things. Instead, see it as chips in a game—not cash, but the tools that let you keep playing. The more you detach from the idea that this is your "hard-earned money," the clearer your decision-making will become.

Of course, you are human, so emotions will always be involved. But when you stop seeing money as something to protect and start viewing it as a resource for calculated risks, the pressure starts to ease. You will stop making impulsive decisions based on fear or excitement, and instead, focus on playing the long-term game. Once you make this shift, something powerful will happen—it will become much easier to press on the gas when the time is right and take trading to the next level.

2. The comfort zone

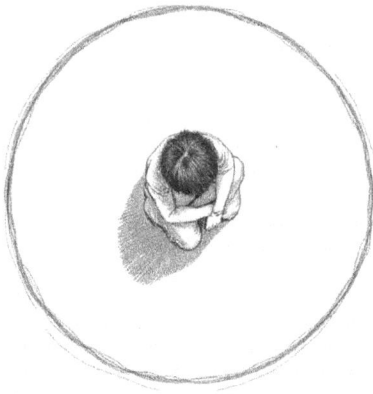

One of the biggest reasons traders struggle to increase their trade size is their comfort zone—that mental space where everything feels safe and under control.

When you trade a size that does not make your heart race, your hands sweat, or your emotions spiral, it feels manageable. You take positions you are used to, work within a risk level that does not stress you out, and everything seems fine. But the moment you think about increasing your size, it suddenly feels like uncharted territory — full of uncertainty and fear.

Trading is not just about having a solid strategy. It is just as much a mental game. You might have the skills, but if you are not willing to push beyond what feels comfortable, you will always be stuck at the same level. Think of a swimmer who is confident in the shallow end but never dares to step into deeper waters. They might be fully capable, but the fear of the unknown keeps them stuck. The same happens with traders. They might handle their current size well, but the thought of increasing it — even slightly — makes them hesitate. This happens because increasing your trade size does not just mean risking more money — it means dealing with a stronger emotional response. The stakes feel higher. The wins feel incredible, almost addictive.

But the losses? They cut deeper than before. It is like turning up the volume on every emotion, and many traders are not prepared for that intensity, so they stay where it feels safe — even if it means limiting their growth.

So how do you break free from this comfort zone? The answer is not to take a massive leap all at once. That would be like our swimmer jumping straight into deep water without preparation. Instead, the key is gradual exposure — small, controlled steps that help you build confidence. If you are used to risking 1% of your capital per trade, try increasing it slightly — to 1.2%, then 1.5%. This way, you ease into the discomfort without overwhelming yourself. Growth is always uncomfortable at first. Think of it like strength training. When you start lifting weights, even the lighter ones feel heavy. But as you keep pushing yourself, your muscles adapt, and those same weights start feeling easier.

The same applies to trading—your mental and emotional muscles grow stronger the more you push beyond what feels safe. Over time, what once felt like a big jump in size just feels like the next logical step.

Another shift that helps is changing how you think about sizing up. Most traders focus on what they could lose instead of what they could gain. They worry about the next trade, the next loss, the next mistake. But trading is not about a single trade—it is a game of probabilities. No single trade should define your success or failure. The key is looking at the bigger picture. If you have a tested strategy with a solid edge, then a few losses along the way do not matter. What matters is sticking to your process and letting the probabilities work in your favour over time. This is where emotional resilience comes into play. It is not just about handling the ups and downs of trading—it is about staying steady no matter what happens.

A simple way to build this resilience is through journaling. Write down your thoughts after each trade—how you felt, what went well, what did not. This helps you spot patterns in your emotions and reactions. Mindfulness techniques can also help. Something as simple as taking deep breaths before placing a trade or visualising different outcomes can make a big difference. The goal is to have a mental framework that keeps you grounded, no matter how volatile the market gets.

Let us talk about losses for a moment—because the fear of losing more money is one of the biggest reasons traders avoid sizing up. It is a real concern, but it is also something that can be reframed. Losses are not something to avoid at all costs. They are part of the process. Every trader experiences losses—it is not about eliminating them, but managing them.

Yes, increasing size means larger losses in absolute terms. But if you are sticking to your risk management rules, the loss is still just a percentage of your account, not something catastrophic. It is the cost of doing business—like paying rent in a regular company.

Another helpful approach is to set clear, measurable goals for increasing size. Instead of randomly deciding when to size up, create specific criteria. Maybe you could increase your size after five consecutive profitable trades or after reaching a certain percentage of growth in your account. Having these milestones takes the guesswork out of the process. It is like following a structured training plan—you know exactly when to push harder and when to hold steady.

Finally, after you have sized up, take time to review and reflect. How did it feel? What challenges came up? What lessons can you take forward? The reflection process helps fine-tune your approach, making it easier to handle even larger sizes in the future.

Stepping out of your comfort zone is not easy, but it is the only way to grow. By taking gradual steps, strengthening your emotional resilience, and keeping your focus on the long-term game, you will find that what once seemed scary becomes manageable. And that is how you level up in trading—one step, one size increase, one trade at a time.

3. You don't trust your system enough

One major reason traders hesitate to increase their position sizes is lack of trust in their trading system. If you do not fully trust your system, how can you trust yourself to execute it with confidence? It is a tricky cycle—one that keeps many traders stuck at lower sizes, afraid to take the next step. But let us break it down with a simple story. Imagine a father who has spent his entire life building a multi-billion-dollar business from scratch. He has poured his heart, time, and energy into making it a success. Now, as he gets older, his son expresses interest in taking over part of the company. But there is a problem — this son has a history of being unreliable. He jumps from one thing to the next, never really committing to anything. He hasn't shown the focus, discipline, or skills needed to handle such a critical responsibility.

Doubt keeps you standing still even when the path is safe.

How do you think the father would feel about handing over an important division of the company to him? Even though he loves his son, he would probably hesitate. Maybe he would start by giving him a smaller, less crucial role — something where failure would not be disastrous — before trusting him with a major part of the business.

This is exactly how you feel about yourself when you have not yet proven that you can trust your trading system. If you have not seen, time and again, that your strategy works, you will hesitate to increase your size. Deep down, you may feel like you are not ready. And that hesitation is not random — it is a result of experience, or rather, the lack of it.

So, how do you build that trust? It does not happen overnight. You cannot just decide to trust your system — you have to give yourself reasons to believe in it. And that starts with backtesting. Backtesting is like running your business model through different scenarios before making real decisions. It lets you test your strategy across various market conditions without risking actual money. You are looking for evidence—proof that your system holds up over time, not just during lucky streaks. A solid strategy should have ups and downs, but an overall positive trajectory. That is what gives you the confidence to trust it in live trading.

But trusting your system is only half the equation. The other half? Trusting yourself to execute it properly. This is where execution discipline comes in. You need to prove to yourself that you can follow your plan, no matter what the market throws at you. Because let us be honest—when real money is on the line, emotions start creeping in. Doubt, fear, greed—they all show up. And if you let them dictate your actions, even the best trading system will not save you. Discipline means sticking to the plan, trade after trade, without letting emotions pull you off course.

So, how do you reach the point where increasing size feels natural? It is a process. You have to earn that confidence step by step.

1. **Master your strategy**: Backtest until you know your system inside out. Understand its strengths, weaknesses, and how it behaves in different conditions.
2. **Focus on execution**: Once you move to live trading, shift your focus from the results of individual trades to following the plan consistently.
3. **Build small wins**: Start small. Prove to yourself that you can stick to the system, even through losses. Confidence comes from seeing reliable execution over time.

As you gain experience, something interesting happens. Your perspective shifts. It is like the father in our story – he sees his son showing up every day, making smart decisions, handling responsibilities with care. Trust is earned, not forced. In trading, as you see your system perform and watch yourself execute it without hesitation, confidence builds naturally.

One day, you will realise that increasing size does not feel scary anymore. It will not feel like a risky leap – it will feel like the next logical step. You will not have to force yourself into it. You will just know that you are ready. In trading, trust is everything. It is what allows you to take bigger risks without fear paralysing you. But trust is not something you can manufacture – it has to be earned through proof and practise. You have to show yourself – through countless trades – that you are capable of handling more.

Just like the father in our story would not hand over his business to someone who has not proven themselves, you should not increase your trade size until you have earned that trust in yourself. But once you do, that next step will not feel like a gamble. It will feel like progress.

4. Give yourself a reason to size up

Let us be clear – do not size up just because you feel like it. Size up when you have earned it. One of the biggest mistakes traders make is randomly deciding to double their position size overnight, thinking it will instantly boost their returns. That is like walking into the gym one day and saying, "You know what? I will lift twice as much weight today!" – without any prior build-up. What happens next? You probably injure yourself. Trading works the same way. You cannot just flip a switch and expect your profits to double. If you want to increase your size, you need to build a cushion first.

That means consistently banking profits over time, creating a buffer in your account. Think of it like setting up a safety net—something to absorb the inevitable bumps and setbacks that come with taking on bigger risks.

WHY A BUFFER MATTERS

When you have this buffer, you can afford to give back some gains to the market, because drawdowns are unavoidable. And here is the thing: when you size up, your drawdowns get bigger in absolute terms.

Imagine losing 5% of a 100K account—it is manageable. But 5% of a 5 crore account? That is a whole different ball game. The losses hit harder, and they are a lot tougher to stomach if you are not prepared.

So, instead of impulsively increasing your size when things are not going well, focus on stacking up profits over several months. Make sure you are in a position where you can absorb a few hits and still stay in the game.

A PRACTICAL APPROACH TO SCALING UP

If you want to be systematic about it, here is a rough guideline. Say you are currently risking 0.5% per trade, and your average drawdown is around 4% on the account level. Before you even think about increasing your size, aim to build at least an 8% profit cushion. That way, if you decide to double your risk, you have got some wiggle room.

But here is the thing: jumping straight from 0.5% risk to 1% per trade is a massive leap. A more sensible approach is to go step by step. Consider adding just 0.1% risk for every

1-2% gain in your account. This way, you are not putting all your eggs in one basket and can adjust smoothly.

THE ART OF SIZING DOWN

Another crucial part of this equation is knowing when to size down. It is easy to get carried away when your equity curve is climbing, but what happens when it starts to dip? If you keep trading at the same size during a rough patch, you are likely to deepen your drawdown. That is why it is important to lower your size when things are not going well, just as you would increase it when they are. Think of it like using cruise control in a car. You speed up when the road is clear, but when you hit traffic, you slow down. This helps you avoid sudden stops—or in trading terms, drastic losses—because your position size adapts to the conditions of your account.

FINE-TUNING YOUR APPROACH

Remember, the process of scaling up should not be rushed. It is not just about numbers; it is also about your mental readiness. Handling bigger sizes means handling bigger emotional swings too. You have to be comfortable seeing larger amounts of money on the line, both in terms of profits and losses. If you find yourself getting anxious or losing sleep over your trades, it might be a sign that you have sized up too quickly. The goal is to gradually stretch your comfort zone, not break it.

So, pay attention to how you feel as you adjust your size. It is better to take smaller, consistent steps forward than to leap ahead and stumble.

CHAPTER SUMMARY

THE VEXING QUESTION OF SCALING UP

emotional attachment

DON'T ASSOCIATE REAL LIFE VALUE WITH TRADE OUTCOMES IT HINDERS OBJECTIVE DECISION MAKING

comfort ZONE

DON'T GET STUCK IN COMFORT ZONE WITH MANAGEABLE RISK DON'T HESITATE TO INCREASE TRADE SIZE

Lack of TRUST in SYSTEM

MAKES IT DIFFICULT FOR TRADERS TO TRUST THEMSELVES WITH LARGER POSITIONS

mindSET

A MINDSET FOCUSSED ON POTENTIAL LOSSES RATHER THAN LONG-TERM GAINS PREVENTS TRADERS FROM SCALING EFFECTIVELY

inadequate RISK MANAGEMENT

VIEW RISK AS MANAGEABLE PART OF PROCESS AND TAKE CALCULATED STEPS TO INCREASE SIZE

LEAVE COMFORT

RISK

TRUST

17

BALANCING LIFE AND TRADING: THE PATH TO TRUE SUCCESS

"Success is not the key to happiness. Happiness is the key to success. If you love what you are doing, you will be successful."
— Albert Schweitzer

We traders often believe that if we get better at trading, our whole life will improve. It sounds simple — make more money, and everything else will fall into place, right?

But real life does not always work like that. Some of the best traders I know were already happy before they started making consistent profits. They did not become happy because they made money; they made money because they were happy. It might sound surprising, but that is how it works. The more you chase something, the harder it becomes to catch. Many traders are so afraid of losing money that they end up doing exactly that—losing money.

The best traders do not trade with fear. They are not sitting at their desks thinking, "If I do not make a big profit this month, I will not be able to pay my bills." They do not let fear control them.

A lot of people treat trading like a salary job, expecting to earn a fixed amount every day or every month. But that is not how the market works. It is called a capital market for a reason, and capital is not just about money—it also includes your mental and emotional strength. When you live a balanced and happy life, you trade with a clear and calm mind. You do not feel desperate or stressed. You stay focused, disciplined, and make decisions with confidence instead of fear. That is what gives you a real edge in trading.

In this section, we will talk about why a good life leads to good trading—not the other way round. We will see how your lifestyle, mindset, and overall happiness can directly impact your success in the market.

Stop thinking that trading success will fix everything. Instead, let us understand how living well can help us become consistently profitable traders.

1. Have an alternative income source

I believe in the potential of the market, but I also know that it is not something you can depend on as your only source of income—unless your trading capital is huge compared to your expenses. The truth is, most people do not have that advantage. Many come from humble backgrounds, which makes it difficult to survive purely on trading income. It is not impossible, but it is risky.

Trading without an alternative income is like free solo climbing—one slip, and there's nothing to catch you

When you rely on trading to pay your bills, your mindset changes. Instead of thinking, "I need to take good trades," you start thinking, "I need to make money." This small shift can hurt your performance.

Even if you have great strategies, the pressure to make money can stop you from trading at your best. I have seen people jump into full-time trading without realising how tough it can be. Sometimes, trading feels easy—you analyse the market, take trades, and everything works perfectly. These good phases can last for months, making traders feel confident enough to quit their jobs. But that is where many go wrong. Just because the market has been easy does not mean it will stay that way. Every trader, no matter how skilled, will face bad phases. Some of these rough patches pass quickly, but others can last for months. If you rely only on trading income without having enough savings, you could end up in serious trouble when the market turns against you.

A good rule to follow if you are thinking about full-time trading: have at least three years' worth of expenses saved up — separate from your trading capital. If you do not have that, it is better to wait. I know many traders who trade part-time and still make steady profits. They do not depend on their trading income, so they can focus on long-term wealth instead of short-term survival. Some even enjoy their jobs and do not want to quit. Of course, not everyone feels the same way. But if you do, keeping your job while growing your trading capital is the safest approach. This way, you will not have to worry about making money from trading every month, and you can perform better in both areas.

If I had to start over, this is exactly what I would do. It might not be what you want to hear, but trust me — I have seen the market when it is kind, and I have seen it when it is brutal. You do not want to be in a weak position when things go wrong.

2. Mould your trading to suit your lifestyle

A well-tailored suit feels effortless because it's made to fit you. Your trading should feel the same—shaped around your life, not forced into someone else's mould.

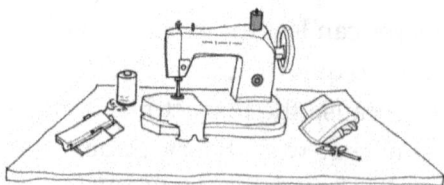

Most people do not realise that their biggest advantage comes from shaping things to fit their life — not the other way around. The real edge is not in copying someone else but in understanding yourself. When you try to imitate others, you are competing in their game, where they already have an upper hand. Instead, focus on your own strengths and weaknesses. Many traders skip this step. They do not take the time to figure out what they are naturally good at, so they miss the chance to build on their strengths. Instead, they keep forcing themselves to improve in areas where they have no natural advantage, which only leads to frustration. This applies to trading just as much as anything else in life.

Every person is different, and that is something you need to accept when deciding how to trade. A 20-year-old with no financial responsibilities can afford to take bigger risks. But someone with a family cannot trade the same way because they have more on the line. If you ask a family person to trade in a fast-paced, high-risk style, they will struggle because they already have too much to manage. On the other hand, if a young person with no obligations is forced to trade in a slow, patient style, they might lose interest and make mistakes. The key is to match your trading style with your life. If you have many daily responsibilities, you might need a trading approach that does not require you to sit in front of the screen all day, monitoring the changes in the market. But if you have free time and can handle more risk, you might prefer an active trading style that needs quick decisions. It is not just about finding time to trade—it is about making sure your trading style suits your personality, lifestyle, and mindset. Your stage in life, your ability to take risks, and even your patience level all influence what kind of trader you can be. Ignoring these things can make trading stressful and ineffective. But when you work with them instead of against them, trading feels smoother and more natural.

246 The Psychology of Trading

This also connects to a bigger idea: building a good life helps you trade better. When your trading style fits your lifestyle, you feel less pressure, stay more focused, and perform better. You do not constantly struggle to balance things—you make trading work for you. This creates a positive cycle: a good life supports good trading, and good trading supports a good life. So take a step back and think about your life, personality, and what you really want from trading. Be honest with yourself about your strengths and weaknesses.

When you do this, you will create a trading style that not only suits your life but also improves it. That is when trading becomes both effective and enjoyable.

3. If you do not enjoy the process, your trading results will reflect it

If you have ever met a trader who makes money consistently, you have probably noticed one thing—they truly enjoy trading.

Many people think top traders are in it just for the money. While money is definitely part of the equation, what really keeps them hooked is the challenge. The best traders love solving problems, thinking creatively, and figuring out things that most people overlook. They do not get carried away by others' opinions, and they know how to take losses without letting them shake their confidence. That is what sets them apart. You might be able to trade for a while without loving the process, but think long-term. Can you see yourself doing this every day for the next 10 or 20 years?

Trading can be boring at times. In fact, the best trading is often boring—there is no constant thrill, no daily excitement. If you do not enjoy the actual work—the research, the strategy-building, the patience—you will struggle to stick with it.

The reality is, if you do not love the process, it will eventually show in your results. Trading is not just about making money; it is about the journey. The best traders find joy in learning, satisfaction in solving challenges, and fulfillment in the daily routine. When you enjoy what you do, you make better decisions, stay disciplined, and have a much better chance at long-term success.

So ask yourself—do you genuinely enjoy trading? If the answer is yes, you are on the right path. If not, it might be time to rethink your approach, because without real passion for the game, staying in it for the long haul will be tough.

4. A healthy body leads to a healthy mindset

Sharpen your body, sharpen your mind because trading, like strength, is built on discipline.

As traders, we always want to stay at the top of our game. We learn from our mistakes, try not to repeat them, and keep pushing ourselves every single day—even on weekends. This never-ending grind does not stop even after you start making money. In the beginning, the learning curve is so steep that most traders put everything they have into it, often burning themselves out.

We all know that having the right mindset is key to trading well. But what we often forget is that when you are exhausted and your mind is cluttered, no mental trick can instantly fix it. The only real solution is to recharge—to take a break, step outside, and give your mind the rest it needs.

Your physical health plays a big role in how you feel mentally. The more you move your body, the better you will feel, and the faster you will be able to clear your mind. Exercise—whether it is a walk, a yoga session, or a proper workout—has a huge impact on your mental state. When you move, your body releases endorphins—natural mood boosters that help reduce stress and improve focus. Exercise also increases blood flow to the brain, sharpening your thinking and helping you stay alert.

Our bodies were not designed to sit and stare at screens all day. For thousands of years, humans were constantly moving—hunting, farming, gathering. But we spend most of our time sitting these days, and that is not what our bodies were built for. This mismatch between how we live and what our bodies need can lead to both physical and mental struggles.

When you make exercise a part of your routine, you align your body and mind with what it is naturally meant to do. This makes you feel more energetic, more focused, and more resilient—qualities every trader needs to handle the ups and downs of the market. So, if you feel drained, lose focus, or struggle with decision-making in your trading, take a step back and check your physical health. Start moving more, and you will likely notice an improvement in your mindset—and in your trading results. A healthy body leads to a healthy mind. And in trading, that can make all the difference.

5. A supportive environment is key to thriving in trading

Success in trading isn't just about skill it's about having people who lift you up when the market pulls you down.

There is a common saying, "A happy wife leads to a happy life." While it might sound like a simple joke, there is actually a deeper truth to it—especially when it comes to trading. Trading is not just about charts and numbers. It is a tough mental game that demands patience, discipline, and emotional stability. If you have a supportive spouse, understanding parents, or even friends who believe in you, your journey becomes much smoother.

Why does this matter? Because trading is full of ups and downs. No matter how skilled you are, you will face losing streaks, self-doubt, and moments of frustration. During those times, having people who support your goals can make a huge difference. Their encouragement helps you stay positive, focused, and motivated—even when the market is not in your favour. Support also means understanding. If your family or partner respects the time and energy you put into trading, you will be able to concentrate without unnecessary stress. They may not fully understand how trading works, but their belief in you can keep you going.

On the other hand, a negative or unsupportive environment can be a major obstacle. Constant doubts, criticism, or distractions can drain your mental energy. It is hard to make smart trading decisions when you are dealing with negativity at home. That is why it is important to create a supportive environment. If you are married or in a relationship, talk to your partner about your trading journey. Share your goals, challenges, and why their support matters. If you live with family, let them know how much their encouragement helps you stay on track. At the end of the day, trading can be a lonely road. The market does not care about your struggles, but having the right people around you can make the journey easier. Just like a healthy body leads to a strong mind, a supportive environment builds the resilience you need to succeed in trading.

6. Know when it is time to walk away

In the end, trading is not for everyone. No matter how exciting or rewarding it may seem, your real strengths might lie elsewhere. Just because others around you are diving into trading does not mean you have to follow the same path. Being honest with yourself is far better than facing regret later. I have seen plenty of young people abandon their studies and careers because they believe trading is their future. But let us be real — the odds of making it in this game are slim. I do not mean to discourage you, just to give you a reality check.

It is easy to get carried away with motivational talk, but reality hits differently when you have spent years trying to succeed, only to feel stuck. Meanwhile, your peers might progress in their careers, leaving you questioning whether you made the right choice. If you think you have what it takes to make it in trading, do not just assume — prove it to yourself first. Test your skills, experience the ups and downs, and see if you genuinely have a knack for this. If not, there is no shame in shifting your focus to something where you truly excel. A fulfilling career is not just about chasing trends—it is about aligning your strengths with what you enjoy. If trading is not that for you, that is completely fine. There are countless other opportunities out there, and real success comes from finding one that truly fits you.

CHAPTER SUMMARY

GOOD LIFE = GOOD TRADING

Happiness FIRST — SUCCESSFUL TRADERS ARE OFTEN HAPPY PEOPLE WHICH CONTRIBUTES TO TRADING SUCCESS

BALANCE IS KEY — BALANCED LIFESTYLE BRINGS CALM AND CLEAR MIND TO TRADING, BETTER DECISIONS REDUCED ANXIETY

ADAPT TRADING TO LIFE — MOLD YOUR TRADING STYLE TO FIT YOUR LIFE CIRCUMSTANCES, RISK TOLERANCE, AND PERSONALITY FOR SUSTAINABLE APPROACH

enjoy THE PROCESS — GENUINE ENJOYMENT OF THE ANALYSIS, STRATEGY AND PATIENCE CRUCIAL FOR LONG-TERM COMMITMENT & SUCCESS

SUPPORTIVE ENVIRONMENT — CONTRIBUTION TO RESILIENCE AND FOCUS NEEDED TO THRIVE IN TRADING

BE HAPPY

ENJOY

SUPPORT

18

THE JOURNEY NEVER ENDS

As we near the end of this book, I want to wrap things up by touching on a topic that is not only crucial in trading but in how we live our lives: our relationship with the journey and the goals we set for ourselves. So often, we get caught up in the chase—focused on hitting those big milestones, making sure we are doing everything we can to reach our goals. It is easy to start thinking that our happiness and success, is tied to the moment we finally achieve our goals. But the thing is, it is not the achievement itself that brings lasting happiness. It is everything that happens along the way—the late nights spent preparing charts, the moments of doubt, the small wins, and even the losses. That is where the real value lies. When you finally hit a goal, there is a brief moment of satisfaction, sure, but then what? The next goal comes into view, and the chase begins again.

The journey never really stops. That is why it is so important to find joy in the process itself—not just in reaching the destination. Hard work should not be something you only do to get out of a tough spot; it should be something you enjoy because you love what you are doing. When you are truly passionate about something, it does not feel like work—it feels like play, even if others see it differently. The key is to develop a mindset that finds fulfilment in the journey, not just in the end result.

Remember, even when you reach your goals, it is not the end of the road—it is just a reset, a chance to start over with new challenges and new opportunities to learn. No matter how good you get, there will always be more to understand and more to master. So approach the market, and life, with an open mind and a willingness to keep learning. You might hit your goals, but it is never the end—it is just the beginning. Enjoy the journey. After all, it is where you will spend 99% of your life.

As you close this book, remember: the journey matters. Your relationship with the process matters. Let that be your guide as you continue, both in trading and in life.

* 9 7 8 9 3 4 9 3 5 8 0 6 5 *